D1395256

A
HEALING
HOUSE
OF
PRAYER

A
HEALING
HOUSE
OF
PRAYER

MORRIS MADDOCKS

Hodder & Stoughton
LONDON SYDNEY AUCKLAND TORONTO

The Scripture quotations in this publication are from The Holy Bible, New International Version, Copyright © 1973, 1978, 1984, by International Bible Society. Published by Hodder & Stoughton Limited. Used by permission.

British Library Cataloguing in Publication Data

Maddocks, Morris
  A healing house of prayer.
  1. Prayers for the sick
  I. Title
  242'.4   BV270

  ISBN 0-340-41036-1

Contents

ROOMS FOR THE MONTH

ROOMS FOR THE CHURCH'S SEASONS

SPARE ROOMS

Introduction

Leslie Weatherhead's beautiful book *A Private House of Prayer* gained a universal welcome as soon as it was published, nearly thirty years ago. During that time it has become a classic and will remain so. Born out of the Methodist tradition it has helped Christians of all denominations to draw nearer to their Lord. Here I am able to speak from experience, for its creative spirituality which meets all occasions, has greatly helped Anne and me, particularly during the 'wilderness' periods of our lives. It has helped to transform those periods into times of preparation and renewal for the next step on the journey. I am certain our experience is far from being unique.

It has therefore been a humbling privilege to be invited by the publishers to write what is more of a companion volume than a successor to *A Private House of Prayer*. As you see, we have chosen to call it *A Healing House of Prayer*.

Books on healing are proliferating at the present time fairly speedily. My own conviction is that the renewal of the Christian healing ministry in our time is a word to the Church. The healing movement has in fact an urgent task to perform within the Church. That task is to recall the Church to a full expression of its healing dimension in evangelism and in pastoral care. The purpose as to which motivates the task is solely one of giving glory to God. The aims of the task will only be fulfilled through a sound basis of prayer.

The healing movement from the beginning of this century has been born out of prayer. Prayer was both the means and the message in the foundation of the healing Guilds. Leslie Weatherhead used to take one name to his congregation of two thousand on a Sunday evening at the City Temple for concentrated prayer. It was his constant experience that blessings came from such saturating prayer. Possibly the greatest contribution the healing movement is making to the life of all the churches in our time is this recalling of Christians to deep prayer.

My own prayer, which Anne shares with me, is that this little book will make a small contribution to the deepening spirituality of the healing movement within all the churches. Such healing prayer is in itself an act of healing for the Church, to the intent that we may all be one, as the Lord of the Church prayed for members of his Body – that we may be a healed Church as well as a healing Church. Perhaps the healing power of Christ will only be fully unleashed when this is so. In the meantime we have the encouragement of healing blessings granted to the quiet, sustained and devoted prayer of ordinary Christians, as well as the blessings given in answer to the more demonstrative types of ministry. Such constant and faithful praying will always yield a harvest of blessings and be the backbone of the healing movement's contribution to the life of the Church. It will therefore assist the Church in its work for the Kingdom, the harvest of a healed creation. For these prayers are the leaves on the tree which Christ ascended for the healing of the nations.

I have tried to preserve these wide themes of prayer to which Leslie Weatherhead gave such skilful treatment; also the various types of prayer such as Affirmation and Adoration, Praise and Thanksgiving, Confession and Forgiveness, Petition and Intercession, and Meditation. I have attempted this by the choice of the seven rooms which I have named as the constant departments for each house or day, but also – and here is an innovation – by giving a theme to each of the thirty-one days of the month. My hope is that this will both concentrate and focus the prayer each day and also be useful at times of public or group prayer, when the leader wants to choose a particular theme. In addition there are 'houses' for some of the major seasons of the Christian year, and I have followed Dr Weatherhead in adding some spare rooms for various prayers to which I hope users of this book will add their own.

For some Christians who are in the most hectic part of their lives, it may not be possible to make the full tour of the house each day. I would recommend them to select two or three rooms, according to their inclination and sit down in them unhurriedly, always ending with *The door into the world*. For the majority I would covet a leisurely stroll through the whole house, erring on the side of spending time in silent moments between the rooms or pausing to contemplate a picture or vision evoked in one particular room. The Lord is usually in the 'still small voice'; he is the 'Go-between God'.

Especially I would hope that this book might be a small adornment on the persons of the caring professions; from working among them I am aware of their increasing search for some spiritual sustenance as a daily diet. As a fellow Christian and colleague in the healing ministry of Christ, I pray this may aid their search.

Anne and I feel that this book has in many ways been a corporate effort, in that we have been conscious of the prayer of many people for the enterprise, especially our Acorn colleagues and supporters, our northern healing prayer fellowship, and other friends in the healing organisations and homes. It seems right that it has all been earthed (and 'heavened' we hope!) in prayer. Some of these people have also kindly offered contributions which are acknowledged below. From all with whom we have worked and prayed we have learned much, and something of this will show in the pages that follow. One special mention must be for Edward England, without whom no pages would follow! It was he who sowed the seeds of the whole idea of this enterprise. For the help of all these people we are deeply grateful.

I should like to offer some suggestions and comments about the use of the book. It is more an aid to praying than the prayer itself. The material you find particularly helpful you may wish to mark for more constant use. The successive dots are an indication for you to add your own petitions or lift up the people for whom you wish to pray to the Lord. The asterisks are indications for silence and prayerful thought, which it is hoped *The quiet room* may especially inspire. The purpose of the book will be lost if it does not help us to pray and be open to God and what he has to give us. He has a healing blessing for each one of us that will the better equip us to fulfil the destiny of his call to us.

Finally, let us have a preliminary stroll through each room:

1 *The entrance to the house of God's glory*

Here we prepare to enter the presence of God and seek a deeper awareness of his glory. Let us begin our praying as we are accustomed to do, whether it is gathering ourselves in silence and stillness, or looking at a crucifix or making the sign of the cross or saying the 'Our Father', or a combination of these ways with any others. It is essential to feel relaxed and yet expectant of the glory that shall be revealed to us in the tiny doses we are able to take.

A long time ago, a doctor said to me, 'I shall never believe in any healing ministry that does not redound to the glory of God.' I have never forgotten this and have often been reminded of it by the pioneers and practitioners of the Christian Healing Ministry who have all been so conscious of the glory of God. I think of Dorothy Kerin; I think of George Bennett who dedicated the new chapel at the Old Rectory, Crowhurst as 'the chapel of Christ's glory'. The purpose of all our praying, the purpose of all our ministry, the purpose of our whole life is nothing other than God's glory, the very nature of God, constantly hymned by the angels in heaven and the whole communion of saints. It is this house of praise, this dimension of holiness, this dazzling light of the eternal glory which we prepare now to enter.

2 *The therapy room*

An awareness of God's glory compels us to see how far we fall short and confronts us with our need for healing and forgiveness. So we enter the Lord's therapy room. He knows the diagnosis and will provide the correct prescription. He will show us what needs to be opened up and dealt with in our lives, and 'faithful is he who calls you, who also will do it.' All we have to do is to present ourselves as we are and he will do the rest.

> Nothing in my hand I bring,
> Simply to thy Cross I cling;
> Naked, come to thee for dress;
> Helpless, look to thee for grace.
> A. M. Toplady

3 *The library*

This room speaks for itself. Have a good read. The passage for the day may lead you to other writings, perhaps in the Scriptures. Hopefully it will also evoke silent thought that turns to prayer.

4 *The music room*

Music – real music – is essentially therapeutic. It is good to have an oasis of music in any house, particularly in God's house. Singing God's praises is a healing activity for it is giving him the glory. You may find you want to burst into song (why not?): the majority of the words chosen in this room are well-known Christian hymns. Or if you have your record player at hand, you may prefer to have a health-giving musical interlude, vocal or instrumental. Or if you play an instrument . . . In whatever way helps, let there be a song or melody in the heart, as is appropriate half way through our praying.

5 *The quiet room*

Here we are more on our own, yes – silent in solitude and stillness, but also more is left to our own initiative in praying. Regard the asterisks as opportunities to be in God's presence, silently waiting upon him, quietly determined not to miss a word that he wants you to hear. This room is rather like the sun lounge or conservatory: it is an opportunity to sunbathe, to bask in the light of God's glorious presence.

Let us 'be still and know . . .'

6 *The living room*

This is the room in which everything happens! We eat here, we watch television, we entertain our friends, the family assembles. It is the opportunity room in the house to care for each other's needs as well as our own. Essentially this is the room of intercession; we welcome everyone, whether it is through the television screen or through the door, to come in and sit down so that we may ask God to heal them and care for them, with us, enfolding us all in his love. So may we all emerge from this *living* room more *alive* in his service.

7 *The door into the world*

In one sense we have never left the world: we are part of it. But we have come apart for a time to be with Jesus on the Mount of Transfiguration, and a tiny bit more of his glory has been revealed to us for our healing and for our nourishment, as we continue the journey for him. As we go forth in his name and with his blessing, may all we meet 'take knowledge of us' that we have been in his company.

May Christ the Healer use this book for his glory and for our healing, and so further his Kingdom.

✠ Morris Maddocks
Salisbury
Feast of St Bartholomew 1986

Acknowledgments and Dedication

I am extremely grateful to my editor, David Wavre, and the publishers, Hodder and Stoughton, as well as to my agent, Edward England, for all their encouragement and painstaking care as the book progressed towards publication.

I wish to thank SPCK for their permission to fulfil this contract and to quote from my books which they have published.

Once again thanks are due to June Hall who, now from a distance across the country, tackled with her usual equanimity some of the typing and most of the retyping of the manuscript.

I also want to thank all who sent in suggestions and contributions, – many of which I have been happy to use; among those who sent in material are:

Sheila Andrewes-Uthwatt, Winifred Apps, Frank Baker, Fred and Mary Belcher, V. L. Clarke, Elizabeth Davies, Anne Eggar, Anna Evans, Russell Hunt, 'J' (Glencairn prayer group), Sue Jeffreys, Sylvia Lake, Roy Lawrence, Maro Laxton, Hedi Limebury, Anne Long, Anne Maddocks, Paddy and Betty Mitchell, James More-Molyneux, Di Mowat, Peg Price, Amy Rogers, Celia Russell, Cicely Small, Christopher Woodard.

Especially do I want to thank my wife, Anne, who has lived the work with me, while we have brought the book to birth during the last fourteen months. My gratitude for her constant love and encouragement is unending. Together we wish to dedicate *A Healing House of Prayer* to the glory of God and in prayer for his blessing on the whole healing movement in all the churches, which holds out a torch of hope for us all in the years that are to come.

✝ Morris Maddocks

Abbreviations

AMR   *Hymns Ancient and Modern Revised*
ASB   *The Alternative Service Book* 1980
BCP   *The Book of Common Prayer*
EH   *English Hymnal*
HBCP *The Hodder Book of Christian Prayers*
HBCQ *The Hodder Book of Christian Quotations*
HFT   *Hymns for Today*
NPP   *New Parish Prayers*, edited by Frank Colquhoun
CPP   *Contemporary Parish Prayers*, edited by Frank Colquhoun
PP   *Parish Prayers* edited by Frank Colquhoun
OBP   *The Oxford Book of Prayer*
SU   *Source Unknown*

Note: Unacknowledged material is by the present writer.

ROOMS
FOR
THE
MONTH

Prayer is the test of everything;
prayer is also the source of everything;
prayer is the driving force of everything;
prayer is also the director of everything.
If prayer is right, everything is right.
For prayer will not allow anything to go wrong.
Theophan the Recluse (1815–94)

DAY 1

ADORATION AND HEALING

1 *The entrance to the house of God's glory*

Praise is inner health made audible.
                Lord teach us to adore.
                        C. S. Lewis

How good it is to sing praises to our God,
    how pleasant and fitting to praise him!
The Lord builds up Jerusalem:
    he gathers the exiles of Israel.
He heals the broken-hearted
    and binds up their wounds.
He grants peace to your borders
    and satisfies you with the finest of wheat.
Praise the Lord.
                        Psalm 147: 1–3, 14, 20

Lift up your hearts: we lift them to the Lord.
Let us give thanks to the Lord our God:
it is right to give him thanks and praise.
It is indeed right, it is our duty and our joy,
at all times and in all places to give you thanks and
    praise,
holy Father, heavenly King, almighty and eternal
    God,
through Jesus Christ your only Son our Lord . . .
Therefore with angels and archangels,
and with all the company of heaven,
we proclaim your great and glorious name,
for ever praising you and saying:

Holy, holy, holy Lord,
God of power and might,
heaven and earth are full of your glory.
Hosanna in the highest.

> The Order for Holy Communion Rite A:
> The Eucharistic Prayer, ASB

Father, as we come to adore you,
    grant us to hear your Word so attentively,
        to experience the power of the Spirit so
        luminously,
that we may be healed inwardly, deeply and
    eternally.   Amen.

> M. M., *The Christian Adventure*, SPCK 1983

2 *The therapy room*

Father, help us to worship you in spirit and in
        truth; that our consciences may be quickened
        by your holiness,
    our minds nourished by your truth,
    our imagination purified by your beauty,
    our hearts opened to your love,
    our wills surrendered to your purpose;
and may all this be gathered up in adoration as we
        ascribe glory, praise and honour to you alone,
        through Jesus Christ our Lord.   Amen.

> Adapted from William Temple, NPP1

3 *The library*

Be joyful always; pray continually; give thanks in all
circumstances, for this is God's will for you in Christ
Jesus.

> 1 Thessalonians 5: 16–18

Christians all over the world are experiencing great things
when they praise God. As they praise the Lord for his love,
they find themselves abiding in his love. As they praise the
Lord that his grace is sufficient, they experience that it is

sufficient. As they praise the Lord for his control over their
lives, they see his control in different parts of their lives. As
they praise the Lord for his gentleness and tenderness, they
sense his gentleness and tenderness. As they praise the
Lord for setting them free, they find new freedom.

Whatever you praise the Lord for, that will increasingly
become your living experience, because the more we focus
on God, the more he meets our needs.

So often it's our attitude, rather than our work, that robs
us of our strength. The joy of the Lord is our strength
(Nehemiah 8:10), and so when we praise the Lord, even
when we find it a costly sacrifice to do so, we are likely to
discover fresh springs welling up within us, refreshing and
strengthening us.

But be prepared for things to go wrong at times. We may
be experiencing great things through the power of praise,
and then something happens and we are brought low and
wonder what God is doing. In that situation we must
simply press on and one day we will come out into the
brightness again – and know the joy of his presence with us
once more.

* * * *

Lord, I offer you now a sacrifice of praise for . . .

* * * *

Am I prepared to obey this verse (of scripture), literally,
starting today?

David Watson, *Through the Year with David Watson*
pp 17f, Hodder 1982

4 *The music room*

There was such beauty in the dappled valley
As hurt the sight, as stabbed the heart to tears.
The gathered loveliness of all the years
Hovered thereover, it seemed eternally
Set for men's joy. Town, Tower, trees, river
Under a royal azure sky for ever
Up-piled with snowy towering bulks of cloud
A herald-day of spring more wonderful

Than her true own. Trumpets cried aloud
In sky, earth, blood; no beast, no clod so dull
But the power felt of the day, and of the giver
Was glad for life, humble at once and proud.
Kyrie Eleison, and Gloria,
Credo, Jubilate, Magnificat:
The whole world gathered strength to praise the day.

Ivor Gurney (1890–1937)

Gurney, whose poetry speaks of Gloucester and the surrounding countryside where he was brought up, was also a talented composer. In his early days he was an articled pupil at the Cathedral under Dr Brewer together with Herbert Howells and Ivor Novello.

Tune me, O Lord, into one harmony
With Thee, one full responsive vibrant chord;
Unto Thy praise, all love and melody,
Tune me, O Lord.

Christina Rossetti (1830–1894)

5 *The quiet room*

The Spirit of the Sovereign Lord is on me,
     because the Lord has anointed me
     to preach good news to the poor.
He has sent me to bind up the broken-hearted,
     to proclaim freedom for the captives
     and release for the prisoners,
to proclaim the year of the Lord's favour
     and the day of vengeance of our God,
to comfort all who mourn,
     and to provide for those who grieve in Zion –
to bestow on them a crown of beauty
     instead of ashes,
the oil of gladness
     instead of mourning,
and a garment of praise
     instead of a spirit of despair.
They will be called oaks of righteousness,
     a planting of the Lord
for the display of his splendour.

Isaiah 61: 1–3

In the Lucan passage, only verse 1 is quoted which, after silence, is followed by Jesus's comment 'Today this scripture is fulfilled in your hearing' (Luke 4: 21). Certainly Jesus filled the role of the Lord's Anointed – the Christ, which is the same word. Certainly he came to proclaim the good news, and his stance was always among the poor. His work of healing was especially of benefit to the broken-hearted, the blind (a better reading than prisoners) and all held captive by 'the world, the flesh and the devil'. The special blessings, however, seem to be reserved for the mourners and those who grieve, those who have had some rough deals in life. They will receive beauty for ashes, the oil of gladness (the name happily given to the oil of healing used by the Roman Catholic laity) for mourning, a garment of praise for a spirit of despair.

This last is a true word of healing. Praise changes the direction of our life, reversing the downward pull, dispelling the oppression from the shadow side of us. It changes us at the centre, because our body immune system is put into top gear and all our reactions are made positive. C. S. Lewis must have experienced this disclosure moment because he once said, 'Praise is inner health made audible.' There would be more positive health and constructive living in our world if people would don 'the garment of praise'. Such people would be the 'oaks of righteousness', the sort of solid and dependable people who have sorted out their relationship with God and with one another. People who spend time in praising God are indeed 'a planting of the Lord for the display of his splendour'. Being attuned to the Lord constantly, they reflect his glory. It was a happy choice of a word of Scripture to herald the beginning of Jesus's ministry.

M. M., *Journey to Wholeness*, pp 29f, SPCK 1986

* * * *

Lord Jesus, Healer and Saviour, I thank you for, and ask for your continuing blessing upon, all who have a share in your healing ministry today:

For doctors who advise and prescribe;
For men and women who nurse;

For surgeons and their teams in operating theatres;
For chemists and laboratory workers in their research;
For hospital porters, cleaners and ambulance staff;
For those who work out diets and prepare them;
For those who give the laying-on-of-hands and anoint
the sick in your name;
For those who meditate and pray.
May they all don *the garment of praise* and be *a true planting
of the Lord for the display of his splendour.*
Give them diligence, give them patience, give them faith;
that their healing work may be a worthy offering of
adoration.
We ask it in your name.   Amen.

After a prayer by William Portsmouth

6 *The living room*

For wholeness for the sick in mind

O Holy Spirit who dost search out all things, even the
deep things of God and the deep things of man, we pray
thee so to penetrate into the springs of personality of all
who are sick in mind, to bring them cleansing, healing
and unity. Sanctify all memory, dispel all fear, and bring
them to love thee with all their mind and will, that they
may be made whole and glorify thee for ever. We ask this
in the Name of him who cast out devils and healed men's
minds, even Jesus Christ our Lord.   Amen.

George Appleton, The Quiet Heart, p 384

Healing in the Church

Bless, O Lord God, your Church in its ministry to the
sick, that it may fulfil your holy will and purpose, and use
all means of grace for the healing of your people; and
grant to those who desire your healing true penitence,
full pardon, and perfect peace; for your dear Son's sake,
Jesus Christ our Lord.   Amen.

Guild of St Raphael

7 *The door into the world*

The more man becomes man, the more he will become
prey to a need, a need that is always more explicit, more
subtle and more magnificent, the need to adore.

Teilhard de Chardin, *Le Milieu Divin*

Then I heard every creature in heaven and on earth and
under the earth and on the sea, and all that is in them,
singing:
  'To him who sits on the throne and to the Lamb
  be praise and honour and glory and power,
      for ever and ever.'
The four living creatures said, 'Amen,' and the elders fell
down and worshipped.

Revelation 5: 13, 14

    Lord, teach us to adore you
        in your glory revealed;
    that in the act of adoration
        we may look up and be healed.   Amen.
                                                    SU
    To God be all glory,
        adoration and worship,
    from the whole Christian people
        on earth and in heaven,
            now and for eternity.   Amen.

DAY 2

A GRATEFUL MEMORY

1 *The entrance to the house of God's glory*

> Give thanks to the Lord, for he is good.
> *His love endures for ever.*
> Give thanks to the God of gods.
> *His love endures for ever.*
> Give thanks to the Lord of lords.
> *His love endures for ever.*
> to him who alone does great wonders,
> *His love endures for ever.*
> who by his understanding made the heavens,
> *His love endures for ever.*
> who spread out the earth upon the waters,
> *His love endures for ever.*
> who made the great lights –
> *His love endures for ever.*
> the sun to govern the day,
> *His love endures for ever.*
> the moon and stars to govern the night,
> *His love endures for ever.*
> Give thanks to the God of heaven.
> *His love endures for ever.*

Psalm 136: 1–9, 26

Gratitude to God makes even a temporal blessing a taste of heaven.

William Romaine, HBCQ G153

Open our eyes, O God, to your glory, that we may worship in spirit and in truth, and offer you the praise of glad and thankful hearts.   Amen.

New Every Morning, p 5, BBC

2 *The therapy room*

Lord Jesus, how can I ever thank you enough for the
amazing gift of your forgiveness?
As I think back over the years, I recall the many times I have
wilfully marred the pattern you had designed for my life;
    the many times I transgressed your commands,

> fell short of your expectations,
> hurt you because I harmed others,
> broke our relationship.

I grieve for ever having offended you.
But each time my faltering penitence was answered by the
free gift of your forgiveness,

> restoring to me the joy of your salvation,
> binding up my sores
> and healing my wounds.

Unworthy as I am, I know myself to be deeply grateful for
the memory of a thousand absolutions,
and for that gift of forgiveness that restored the joy in life.
May all glory, all love, all thanksgiving, be to you for ever,
    my merciful Healer and Redeemer,
        Jesus Christ, my Lord and my God.   Amen.

3 *The library*

In these passages, Father Bernard shows us that the
Eucharist is the *grateful memory* of the Body of Christ and its
members, and how it provides the motivation for a caring-
healing ministry:

The Eucharist is a memorial celebration through which
we meet Christ in grateful remembrance of how he
reached out to the outcast and the sick while proclaiming
the Good News. Through *a grateful memory* we live in the
presence of Christ and experience, in faith, how he
identified and still identifies himself with our sufferings
and with a sick humanity. When, in this memorial, we

praise him for having borne our burden, he inscribes in our hearts and memories his mandate to bear a part of the burden of others, especially of the sick. Thus, we participate in his caring-healing ministry . . .

A 'eucharistic memory', filled with praise for the wondrous deeds of God and thankfulness for all his gifts and all our experiences with gracious people, is an inexhaustible source of health and healing, and perhaps the best contribution to the work of peace at all levels. Christ, the Good Shepherd, the Healer, our Peace, has taught us this clearly and emphatically. We can only wonder why we are such poor learners in this field while learning so easily many less important facts . . .

In Christ and in the Church, the Eucharist is the central and most fruitful sacrament of the saving-healing grace of God. It is also a principal sign of 'forgiveness of sins', of healing hurt memories, a source of peace and an energizing resource for the peace-mission of all Christians. The Eucharist is an efficacious sign of healing faith, hope and love that enables the community and each believer to radiate wholeness and peace, to serve the poor, to care for the sick and to heal the depressed and the anguished. When rightly celebrated, it communicates that joy in the Lord which is a source of strength and health . . .

A truly Eucharistic, *grateful memory* will help us to say our responsible 'Amen' when the need of others appeals to us for our active love. The creative, healing, caring solidarity of the Christian community with the sick and suffering is an integral dimension of the Eucharistic memorial and of a faith-filled memory bearing fruit in caring, healing love.

Bernard Häring CSSR, *Healing and Revealing*, pp 22, 58f
St Paul Publications 1984

4 *The music room*

Speak to one another with psalms, hymns and spiritual songs. Sing and make music in your heart to the Lord, always giving thanks to God the Father for everything, in the name of our Lord Jesus Christ.

Ephesians 5: 19, 20

Now thank we all our God,
With heart and hands and voices,
Who wondrous things hath done,
In whom his world rejoices;
Who from our mother's arms,
Hath blessed us on our way
With countless gifts of love,
And still is ours to-day.

O may this bounteous God
Through all our life be near us,
With ever joyful hearts
And blessèd peace to cheer us;
And keep us in his grace,
And guide us when perplexed,
And free us from all ills
In this world and the next.

All praise and thanks to God
The Father now be given,
The Son, and him who reigns
With them in highest heaven,
The one eternal God,
Whom earth and heaven adore,
For thus it was, is now,
And shall be evermore.
M. Rinkart, Translated Catherine
M. Rinkart, Translated Catherine Winkworth,
AMR 379

5 *The quiet room*

I THANK Thee, God, that I have lived
In this great world and known its many joys;
The song of birds, the strong sweet scent of hay
And cooling breezes in the secret dusk,
The flaming sunsets at the close of day,
Hills, and the lonely, heather-covered moors,
Music at night, and moonlight on the sea,
The beat of waves upon the rocky shore
And wild, white spray, flung high in ecstasy:
The faithful eyes of dogs, and treasured books,
The love of kin and fellowship of friends,

And all that makes life dear and beautiful.
I thank Thee, too, that there has come to me
A little sorrow and, sometimes, defeat,
A little heartache and the loneliness
That comes with parting, and the word, 'Goodbye,'
Dawn breaking after dreary hours of pain,
When I discovered that night's gloom *must* yield
And morning light break through to me again.
Because of these and other blessings poured
Unasked upon my wondering head,
Because I know that there is yet to come
An even richer and more glorious life,
And most of all, because Thine only Son
Once sacrificed life's loveliness for me –
I thank Thee, God, that I have lived.

Elizabeth Craven
Leslie Weatherhead,
A Private House of Prayer, Day 14 Room 2

* * * *

Lord I have so many memories for which I am truly grateful – people, occasions, places, experiences . . . I now want to offer my heartfelt gratitude to you for . . .

6 *The living room*

Almighty God, Father of all mercies, we thine unworthy servants do give thee most humble and hearty thanks for all thy goodness and loving-kindness to us, and to all men; We bless thee for our creation, preservation, and all the blessings of this life; but above all, for thine inestimable love in the redemption of the world by our Lord Jesus Christ; for the means of grace, and for the hope of glory. And, we beseech thee, give us that due sense of all thy mercies, that our hearts may be unfeignedly thankful, and that we shew forth thy praise, not only with our lips, but in our lives; by giving up ourselves to thy service, and by walking before thee in holiness and righteousness all our days; through Jesus Christ our Lord, to whom with thee and the Holy Ghost be all honour and glory, world without end.   Amen.

The General Thanksgiving, BCP

Let us *today* make a specific act of gratitude for . . .

* * * *

> Lift up your hearts.
> We lift them up unto the Lord.
> Let us give thanks unto our Lord God.
> It is meet and right so to do.

It is very meet, right, and our bounden duty, that we should at all times, and in all places, give thanks unto thee, O Lord, Holy Father, Almighty, Everlasting God.
Therefore with Angels and Archangels, and with all the company of heaven, we laud and magnify thy glorious Name; evermore praising thee, and saying,
Holy, holy, holy, Lord God of hosts, heaven and earth are full of thy glory: Glory be to thee, O Lord most High.   Amen.

The Holy Communion service, BCP

7 *The door into the world*

> Give thanks to the Lord, call on his name;
> > make known among the nations what he has
> > > done.
> Sing to him, sing praise to him;
> > tell of all his wonderful acts.
> Glory in his holy name;
> > let the hearts of those who seek the Lord rejoice.
> Look to the Lord and his strength;
> > seek his face always.

Psalm 105: 1–4

One of (the lepers), when he saw he was healed, came back, praising God in a loud voice. He threw himself at Jesus' feet and thanked him – and he was a Samaritan.

Jesus asked, 'Were not all ten cleansed? Where are the other nine? Was no-one found to return and give praise to God except this foreigner?' Then he said to him, 'Rise and go; your faith has made you well.'

Luke 17: 15–19

O God of love, we ask you to give us love:
   love in our thinking,
   love in our speaking,
   love in our doing,
and give us always a grateful and loving memory.
   Amen.

After a prayer by William Temple, NPP 560

Lord, go with us this day and every day.   Amen.

DAY 3

ANOINTED OF GOD

1 *The entrance to the house of God's glory*

> But a Samaritan, as he travelled, came where the man was; and when he saw him, he took pity on him. He went to him and bandaged his wounds, pouring on oil and wine. Then he put the man on his own donkey, brought him to an inn and took care of him.
>
> Luke 10: 33, 34

We can see the person of Christ in the Good Samaritan, coming to us at the precise point where we are now and ministering to us in our present predicament. And when he has healed us, only he can set us on the right way, *his* way.

But the person of Christ is also to be seen in the wounded traveller. When we stop to help someone in dire need, we may find the Christ in that person. That is why we constantly feel that the sick and disabled actually minister to us. They do. *He* does!

Come, Anointed of God, and pour your oil of healing on this wounded traveller, your cleansing wine on any part that is festering; bind up my wounds and set me on *your* way. So that, healed through your anointing, I may minister your healing balm to others struggling on their way, and lead them to *yours*; through your anointing grace, my Lord Saviour and Healer, Jesus Christ-the-Anointed-One. Amen.

2 *The therapy room*

Is any one of you in trouble? He should pray. Is anyone happy? Let him sing songs of praise. Is any one of you sick? He should call the elders of the church to pray over him and *anoint him with oil* in the name of the Lord. And the prayer offered in faith will make the sick person well; the Lord will raise him up. If he has sinned, he will be forgiven. Therefore confess your sins to each other and pray for each other so that you may be healed. The prayer of a righteous man is powerful and effective.

James 5: 13–16

As with visible oil your body outwardly is anointed, so our heavenly Father, Almighty God, grant of his infinite goodness that your soul inwardly may be anointed with the Holy Ghost, who is the Spirit of all strength, relief and gladness. May he, according to his blessed will, restore to you full strength and health of body, mind and spirit that you may withstand all temptations and in Christ's victory triumph over evil, sin and death: Through Jesus Christ our Lord, who by his death has overcome the prince of death; and with the Father and the Holy Spirit evermore lives and reigns, God, world without end.   Amen.

The sacrament of anointing, Western Rite

3 *The library*

I believe, O merciful Jesus, that thou art Christ the true Messiah, the anointed of the Lord, the promised seed, 'which was to bruise the serpent's head', long expected by the fathers, foretold by the prophets, represented by types, which were all fulfilled in thee, O thou the desire of all the nations: all love, all glory, be to thee.
I believe, that thou, O Jesus, wert anointed with the Holy Spirit, that all his gifts and graces were poured out, and diffused like a sweet ointment on thy soul, without measure; thou art altogether lovely, O Christ, and of thy fulness we all receive: all love, all glory, be to thee.
I believe, O thou Anointed of God, that as kings, and priests, and prophets were heretofore anointed with material oil; so by thy heavenly anointing, thou wast

consecrated to be our Prophet, our King, and our Priest,
and in all those three offices, to manifest thy love to us;
and therefore, all love, all glory, be to thee.

Glory be to thee, O Christ, our Prophet, who didst teach,
and reveal, and interpret thy Father's will, and all saving
truth, to the world.

Glory be to thee, O Christ, our King, who dost give laws
to thy people, dost govern and protect us, and hast
subdued all our ghostly enemies.

Glory be to thee, O Christ, our Priest, who dost bless us,
who didst offer thyself a sacrifice, and dost still 'Make
intercession for us'.

Our redemption, our illumination, our support, is
wholly from thy love, O thou anointed of God: all love, all
glory, be to thee.

Thomas Ken, Bishop of Bath and Wells (1637–1711),
An Exposition of the Church Catechism

4 The music room

Hail to the Lord's Anointed,
  Great David's greater Son!
Hail, in the time appointed,
  His reign on earth begun!
He comes to break oppression,
  To set the captive free,
To take away transgression,
  And rule in equity.

He comes with succour speedy
  To those who suffer wrong;
To help the poor and needy,
  And bid the weak be strong;
To give them songs for sighing,
  Their darkness turn to light,
Whose souls, condemned and dying,
  Were precious in his sight.

He shall come down like showers
  Upon the fruitful earth,
And love, joy, hope, like flowers,
  Spring in his path to birth;
Before him on the mountains

Shall peace, the herald, go;
And righteousness in fountains
From hill to valley flow.

Kings shall bow down before him,
And gold and incense bring;
All nations shall adore him,
His praise all people sing:
To him shall prayer unceasing
And daily vows ascend;
His kingdom still increasing,
A kingdom without end.

O'er every foe victorious,
He on his throne shall rest;
From age to age more glorious,
All-blessing and all-blest:
The tide of time shall never
His covenant remove;
His name shall stand for ever,
His changeless name of Love.

J. Montgomery
Set to the tune 'Cruger' composed by
J. Cruger (1598–1662), AMR 219

5 *The quiet room*

I have often pondered quietly on some of my case histories,
from which I have learned so much. I recall a particular one
when I came to realise how the sacrament of anointing can
forge a most powerful contact with our Creator and all that
is best in his creation:

C. was a busy member of Parliament whose mother was
dying of cancer in the north of England. I told him I
should like her to receive the healing sacraments of the
Church, but I would wait until he could leave the House
to come to her bedside. I well remember how we battled
our way to the hospital through a snow storm. His
mother looked pathetically frail as the disease had taken
its toll. So recently she had been a robust, fine looking
woman, actively campaigning for him, supportive of so
much in public life and always surrounded by many

friends and adoring grandchildren. Now we viewed her in the extremity of human weakness. He knelt down at her bedside while I anointed her. I never cease to wonder at the majestic brevity and beauty of the rite of anointing nor at the peace which invariably accompanies the 'celebration' of this sacrament of healing. E. was to die a week later, but a very remarkable thing happened during her last week. She seemed to be separated from her disease and became her 'old self'. It was as if a healing force of explosive energy had effected this transform-ation internally for she sat up, demanded menus and winelists and had many farewell parties for her friends, presiding over them as she used to do in her home. She seemed to be enjoying the anticipation of the banquet in the Kingdom. Her work done and her farewells over, she died in peace.

Her son later wrote to say that never before had he experienced such a nearness to his Creator and to all that was good in creation as when he had been kneeling at his mother's bedside during her anointing. He had been given a glimpse of the things that belong unto his true health, that communication with the divine centre of all being, the Creator of the universe whom we call God.

M.M., The Christian Healing Ministry,
pp 5f, SPCK 1981

*   *   *   *

Let us experience that 'nearness to our Creator and to all that is good in creation.'
Let us seek 'a glimpse of the things that belong unto our true health.'

*   *   *   *

> Teach me, my God and King
> In all things thee to see;
> And what I do in anything,
> To do it as for thee.
> George Herbert (1593–1633)

6 The living room

'The Little Way of Prayer'
Let us, by an act of the will place ourselves in the

presence of Our Divine Lord, and with an act of faith, ask
that He will empty us of self and of ALL desire save that
His Most Blessed Will may be done, and that it may
illumine our hearts and minds. We can then gather
together all those for whom our prayers have been asked,
and hold them silently up to Him, making no special
request – neither asking nor beseeching – but just resting,
with them, IN Him, desiring nothing but that Our Lord
may be glorified in them . . .

In this most simple way of approach He does make
known His Most Blessed Will for us.

Dorothy Kerin, The Burrswood Healing Service
(Quoted by Johanna Ernest in *The Life of Dorothy Kerin*,
Dorothy Kerin Trust 1983)

7 *The door into the world*

Heavenly Father,
you anointed your Son Jesus Christ
   with the Holy Spirit and with power
to bring to man the blessings of your kingdom.
Anoint your Church with the same Holy Spirit,
that we who share in his suffering and his victory
may bear witness to the gospel of salvation;
   through Jesus Christ our Lord.   Amen.

The almighty Lord, who is a strong tower to all who put
their trust in him, be now and evermore *our* defence, and
make *us* believe and trust that the only name under
heaven given for health and salvation is the name of our
Lord Jesus Christ.   Amen.

Ministry to the Sick (Authorised Alternative Services)

The Lord bless *us* and watch over *us*,
The Lord make his face to shine upon *us*
   and be gracious to *us*,
The Lord look kindly on *us* and give *us* peace;
and the blessing of God Almighty,
the Father, the Son, and the Holy Spirit,
be among *us* and remain with *us* always.   Amen.

from The Alternative Service Book 1980

DAY 4

'A TIME TO DIE'

1 *The entrance to the house of God's glory*

They went to a place called Gethsemane, and Jesus said
to his disciples, 'Sit here while I pray.' He took Peter,
James and John along with him, and he began to be
deeply distressed and troubled. 'My soul is overwhelmed with sorrow to the point of death,' he said to
them, 'Stay here and keep watch.'

Going a little further, he fell to the ground and prayed
that if possible the hour might pass from him. '*Abba*,
Father,' he said, 'everything is possible for you. Take this
cup from me. Yet not what I will, but what you will.'

Mark 14: 32–36

On the day when death will knock at my door what shall I
offer him, either in the closing minutes of this life or in the
opening minutes of my new birth in the life beyond? Oh,
I will set before him all the lovely things that I have seen,
all the love that I have received and given, all the insights
of truth that I have gathered, all the things that I have
valued and enjoyed, all the tasks completed or left for
others, all my gratitude and love for the past, all my
content in the present and my hope for the future. Above
all I will offer my recognition of the Lord who has come in
the guise of death, to lead me to the home he has
prepared for me.

Inspired by Rabindranath Tagore
George Appleton, *Journey for a Soul*, Collins/Fontana 1974

O Lord, the first and the last,
the beginning and the end:
you who were with us at our birth,
   be with us through our life;
you who are with us through our life,
   be with us at our death;
and because your mercy will not leave us then,
   grant that we die not,
     but rise to the life everlasting.   Amen.
New Every Morning, p 123, BBC 1973

2 *The therapy room*

Lord, as my mortal hours run by,
   help me to die to the flesh, die to myself,
   die to all that is not of thy Spirit,
     die daily.
So that I may make the last surrender of this life,
   not to death, but to GOD.

Give my soul hunger for its remaking
   by its Beloved, in light:
and bring me to the finishing of faith,
   to my own Easter day,
     IN THEE.

*   *   *   *

O Make my life, O Lord, to its very end
   rehearse melodies for heaven!
Let truth sing in my soul
   and love frame new descants,
     be they never so simple, so faint,
   to the eternal chorus,
     Alleluia, Alleluia, Alleluia.
Eric Milner-White, *My God, My Glory*,
pp 188, 189, SPCK 1954

3 *The library*

I have become more vulnerable as I try to offer more real and therefore more costly friendship. Dying is hard, and friendship with those who are dying is hard too. The demands are those laid on the disciples in the garden of Gethsemane: 'watch with me' (Matthew 26: 38). At the time of crisis I am asked to share the patient's mental suffering, and to feel naked and helpless in the face of death. If ever there comes a time when I find terminal care straightforward, that is the signal for me to leave medicine and take up market gardening. If ever it becomes easy, then I can be sure that I am no longer of any use to my patients . . .

(In times of tiredness and stress) I turn to the Bible, to David's Psalms, and discover a principle that when emotionally shell-shocked by the battles of life, I should vent my frustration and anger on God. There are some who say: 'Oh no! we must never be angry with God.' For David, described as a man after God's own heart, and for me, there was and is no other way. I did not ask to be born. I did not ask to be a hospice doctor. I cannot cope with so much negativity. *Damn it, God, I cannot cope!* There is so much suffering, so much apparent unfairness. Yet on God's desk there is a framed statement. It says quite simply: the buck stops here. As someone said, 'If God had been Prime Minister, he would have been forced to resign aeons ago.'

Being angry with God is a necessity for me. Without this avenue of release, I could not continue as a hospice physician. I am still learning from David. Using his words to hang my anger on undoubtedly helps even though our circumstances are very different.

Be gracious to me, O Lord, for I am in distress,
    and my eyes are dimmed with grief.
My life is worn away with sorrow
    and my years with sighing;
Strong as I am, I stumble under my load of misery;
    there is disease in all my bones.
I have such enemies that all men scorn me;
    my neighbours find me a burden,
    my friends shudder at me;

when they see me in the street they turn quickly
    away.
I am forgotten, like a dead man out of mind.
I have come to be like something lost.

Psalm 31: 9–12

The Psalms I find most helpful are those that express
weariness of spirit as well as more obvious anger. It is not
just the former I identify with: I need to be angry too. And
to thank God that, in his infinite capacity to love and to
give, he is able to absorb all my anger – and more.

Robert G. Twycross, Consultant Physician,
Sir Michael Sobell House Hospice, Oxford, A Time to Die,
Christian Medical Fellowship 1984

4 *The music room*

Abide with me; fast falls the eventide;
The darkness deepens; Lord, with me abide!
When other helpers fail, and comforts flee,
Help of the helpless, O abide with me.

Swift to its close ebbs out life's little day;
Earth's joys grow dim, its glories pass away;
Change and decay in all around I see;
O thou who changest not, abide with me.

I need thy presence every passing hour;
What but thy grace can foil the tempter's power?
Who like thyself my guide and stay can be?
Through cloud and sunshine, O abide with me.

I fear no foe with thee at hand to bless;
Ills have no weight, and tears no bitterness.
Where is death's sting? where, grave, thy victory?
I triumph still, if thou abide with me.

Hold thou thy Cross before my closing eyes;
Shine through the gloom, and point me to the
    skies;
Heaven's morning breaks, and earth's vain
    shadows flee;
In life, in death, O Lord, abide with me!

H. F. Lyte (1793–1847), EH 363

W. H. Monk (1823–1889) who wrote the tune for this hymn – 'Eventide' – had a great gift of composing music that interpreted the words. This hymn has brought healing to many – at funerals, on Remembrance Sunday and even at football matches.

5 *The quiet room*

Remembering our theme, let us slowly recite this favourite psalm of David, absorbing its message into our inner consciousness:

> The LORD is my shepherd, I shall lack nothing.
>> He makes me lie down in green pastures,
> he leads me beside quiet waters,
>> he restores my soul.
> He guides me in paths of righteousness
>> for his name's sake.
> Even though I walk
>> through the valley of the shadow of death,
> I will fear no evil,
>> for you are with me;
> your rod and your staff,
>> they comfort me.
> You prepare a table before me
>> in the presence of my enemies.
> You anoint my head with oil;
>> my cup overflows.
> Surely goodness and love will follow me
>> all the days of my life,
> and I will dwell in the house of the LORD
>> for ever.
>
> Psalm 23

* * * *

O Lord Jesus Christ, who in your last agony did commend your Spirit into the hands of your heavenly Father, have mercy upon all sick and dying persons; may death be unto them the final healing, the gate of everlasting life. Grant them at the last the assurance that whether we wake or sleep we are still at peace in your presence, who is alive and reigns with the Father and the Holy Spirit, one God, for evermore.   Amen.

Adapted from a prayer in the Sarum Primer

6 *The living room*

From a prayer to the risen Lord to accept the cross in life and in death:

Now that I have found the joy of utilizing all forms of growth to make you, or let you, O God, grow in me, grant that I may willingly consent to this last phase of communion in the course of which I shall possess you by diminishing in you . . .

When the signs of age begin to mark my body (and still more when they touch my mind); when the ill that is to diminish me or carry me off strikes from without or is born within me; when the painful moment comes in which I suddenly awaken to the fact that I am ill or growing old; and above all at that last moment when I feel I am losing hold of myself and am absolutely passive within the hands of the great unknown forces that have formed me; in all those dark moments, O God, grant that I may understand that it is you who are painfully parting the fibres of my being in order to penetrate to the very marrow of my substance and bear me away within yourself . . .

The more the future opens before me like some dizzy abyss or dark tunnel, the more confident I may be – if I venture forward on the strength of your word – of losing myself and surrendering myself in you, of being assimilated by your body, Jesus.

Teach me *to treat my death as an act of communion*.

Teilhard de Chardin, Le Milieu Divin

Bring us, O Lord God, at our last awakening into the house and gate of heaven, to enter into that gate and dwell in that house, where there shall be no darkness nor dazzling, but one equal light; no noise nor silence, but one equal music; no fears nor hopes, but one equal possession; no ends nor beginnings, but one equal eternity; in the habitations of thy glory and dominion, world without end.   Amen.

John Donne (1572–1631)

7 The door into the world

God be in my head,
  And in my understanding;

God be in my eyes,
  And in my looking;

God be in my mouth,
  And in my speaking;

God be at my end,
  And at my departing.
Pynson's *Horae*, 1515, AMR 332

I heard a voice from heaven, saying, 'Write this: "Happy are the dead who die in the faith of Christ! Henceforth," says the Spirit, "they may rest from their labours; for they take with them the record of their deeds."'

Revelation 14:13

May the divine assistance remain with us always, and may the souls of the faithful departed, through the mercy of God, rest in peace and rise in glory.   Amen.

DAY 5

A TRUSTING FAITH

1 *The entrance to the house of God's glory*

He who dwells in the shelter of the Most High
    will rest in the shadow of the Almighty.
I will say of the Lord, 'He is my refuge and my
    fortress,
    my God, in whom I trust.'

'Because he loves me,' says the Lord,
    'I will rescue him;
I will protect him, for he
    acknowledges my name.
He will call upon me, and I will answer him;
    I will be with him in trouble,
    I will deliver him and honour him.
With long life will I satisfy him
    and show him my salvation.'

Psalm 91: 1, 2, 14–16

Father, I pray that today I may know with keener awareness that I am in your hands. Well or ill, happy or sad, at
work or at leisure, with others or alone, may I become
increasingly conscious that you, who have called me, are
utterly trustworthy and will accomplish your purpose in
me. Grant me the sense of your presence, born of your
indwelling and enfolding love.

    If this day brings storm or stress, fear or sorrow, pain or
disappointment, or if it brings gladness, serenity, happiness and peace, let nothing rob me of the joy of knowing
I am yours, *kept by your power* in readiness for the coming
of our Lord Jesus Christ.   Amen.

Leslie Weatherhead, A Private House of Prayer

2 The therapy room

Lord, I have been a prisoner
Unwilling to be freed from self and sin,
From prejudice, hypocrisy and vain inglorious
    pride,
From thinking I knew best about so many things.

Lord, forgive your foolish one,
Forgive his words, his deeds, his thoughts,
His careless disregard of you,
His selfish disregard of fellow man.

Lord, I know that I am free,
Yet I lie prone as though in fetters still;
O help me rise! And *give me trust*
To go with you. Amen.

Frank Baker

3 The library

Wednesday, 24 May: In the evening I went very unwill-
ingly to a society in Aldersgate-street, where one was
reading Luther's preface to the Epistle to the Romans.
About a quarter before nine, while he was describing the
change which God works in the heart through faith in
Christ, *I felt my heart strangely warmed.* I felt I did trust in
Christ, Christ alone, for salvation: and an assurance was
given me, that he had taken away my sins, even mine,
and saved me from the law of sin and death.

I began to pray with all my might for those who had in
a more especial manner despitefully used me and persecuted me. I then testified openly to all there, what I
now first felt in my heart. But it was not long before the
enemy suggested, 'This cannot be faith; for where is thy
joy?' Then was I taught, that peace and victory over sin
are essential to faith in the Captain of our salvation; but
that, as to the transports of joy that usually attend the
beginning of it, especially in those who have mourned
deeply, God sometimes giveth, sometimes withholdeth
them, according to the counsels of his own will.

After my return home, I was much besetted with

temptations; but cried out, and they fled away. They returned again and again. I as often lifted up my eyes, and he 'sent me help from his holy place.' And herein I found the difference between this and my former state chiefly consisted. I was striving, yea, fighting with all my might under the law, as well as under grace. But then I was sometimes, if not often, conquered; now, I was always conqueror.

Thursday 25: The moment I awaked, 'Jesus Master,' was in my heart and in my mouth; and I found all my strength lay in keeping my eye fixed upon him, and my soul waiting on him continually.

John Wesley, Diary for 1738

Note: He died in 1791 and is commemorated on May 24th, together with his brother Charles, the great hymn writer.

4 *The music room*

Firmly I believe and truly
   God is Three and God is One;
And I next acknowledge duly
   Manhood taken by the Son.

And I trust and hope must fully
   In that Manhood crucified;
And each thought and deed unruly
   Do to death, as he has died.

Simply to his grace and wholly
   Light and life and strength belong,
And I love supremely, solely,
   Him the Holy, him the Strong.

And I hold in veneration,
   for the love of him alone,
Holy Church as his creation,
   And her teachings as his own.

Adoration ay be given,
   With and through the angelic host,
To the God of earth and heaven,
   Father, Son, and Holy Ghost.

J. H. Newman (1801–1890), AMR 186

5 *The quiet room*

A few days later, when Jesus again entered Capernaum, the people heard that he had come home. So many gathered that there was no room left, not even outside the door, and he preached the word to them. Some men came, bringing to him a paralytic, carried by four of them. Since they could not get him to Jesus because of the crowd, they made an opening in the roof above Jesus and, after digging through it, lowered the mat the paralysed man was lying on. When Jesus saw their faith, he said to the paralytic, 'Son, your sins are forgiven.'

Now some teachers of the law were sitting there, thinking to themselves, 'Why does this fellow talk like that? He's blaspheming! Who can forgive sins but God alone?'

Immediately Jesus knew in his spirit that this was what they were thinking in their hearts, and he said to them, 'Why are you thinking these things? Which is easier: to say to the paralytic, "Your sins are forgiven," or to say, "Get up, take your mat and walk"? But that you may know that the Son of Man has authority on earth to forgive sins . . .' He said to the paralytic, 'I tell you, get up, take your mat and go home.' He got up, took his mat and walked out in full view of them all. This amazed everyone and they praised God, saying, 'We have never seen anything like this!'

Mark 2: 1–12

Here is a profoundly biblical and Christian story, first because it is so personal. Jesus notices *the faith of the four friends* and accepts their energy and ingenuity in seeking God's help for the sick man. They have in fact made the perfect act of intercession, bringing their friend into the presence of Jesus, who responds by treating the man's plight not merely as physical sickness but as the symptom of a deeper sickness. He offers him freedom from the bondage of sin. Remission is here a stronger translation than forgiveness. 'The remission of sins is the total gift of salvation of which physical healing is a part' (R. H. Fuller). It is this deep healing which Jesus came to bring to a fallen race and, as the insertion in the story explains, the Son of Man *has* authority on earth to remit sins. This is part of the Good News and prepares men and women for the Kingdom, by making available in advance the blessings of 'the life of the world to come', that perfect shalom.

Finally the crowd glorifies God, by which Mark means us to notice that Jesus is the person in whom God acts. This would provide additional encouragement for the early Christian community in which the Gospel was written: God still does through word and sacrament what Jesus did in the days of his flesh. Let the Church today also take this lesson to heart.

M. M., *The Christian Healing Ministry*, pp 37f

Lord Jesus, give your Church today *a trusting faith* in your power to heal. In your name we ask it.   Amen.

6 *The living room*

Today let us thank God for those who have gone before us, who by trusting in him totally, experienced the healing power of his love in their lives. We pray that like grace may be available to us:

Father in heaven, we thank you for the witness
        of countless men and women
    who have put their trust in you and found
        unfailing
            power and love.
We pray that your Spirit may give us grace
    when burdened with difficulties,
        to trust in your strength;
    when overwhelmed with sorrow,
        to rest in your love;
    when emptied of feeling and purpose,
        to know you are present;
    after the example of our Saviour Jesus Christ,
        who through the utmost suffering of body,
            agony of mind and darkness of soul,
        still trusted in you.   Amen.

New Every Morning, p 63, BBC

We thank you, our Father, that our loved ones who have
gone from our sight are in your keeping.
Help us to leave them there in perfect trust, because you
love them and us with infinite love.
Grant that we may learn to know you better, so that we
may meet them again in your presence, through faith in
him who loved us and gave himself for us, Jesus Christ
our Saviour.   Amen.

R. E. Cleeve, CPP 631

7 *The door into the world*

This is the victory that has overcome the world, even our
faith. Who is it that overcomes the world? Only he who
believes that Jesus is the Son of God.

1 John 5: 4, 5

Give us, O Lord, so firm a faith in your fatherly love and
wisdom that we may be lifted above our anxieties and
fears, and face the life of each day, and all the unknown
future, with a courageous and quiet spirit.   Amen.
Father, enable us this day to walk trustfully as your
children, giving glory to our Lord Jesus Christ and rejoicing in the power of the Holy Spirit.   Amen.

New Every Morning, BBC, p 61

Lord, may we live in faith,
    walk in love,
    and be renewed in hope,
until the world reflects your glory
    and you are all in all.   Amen.

NPP 28

DAY 6

'BY HIS WOUNDS WE ARE HEALED'

1 *The entrance to the house of God's glory*

He was pierced for our transgressions
    he was crushed for our iniquities;
the punishment that brought us peace was upon him,
    and by his wounds we are healed.

Isaiah 53: 5

The healing of his seamless dress,
    Is by our beds of pain;
We touch him in life's throng and press,
    And we are whole again.

J. G. Whittier (1807–92), EH 408

Lord, we thank and praise you that your wounds have brought our healing. May this time of prayer continue this transformation of our lives into an instrument of healing for your glory. In your name we ask it.   Amen.

2 *The therapy room*

The cry of earth's anguish went up unto God,
    Lord, take away pain!
The shadow that darkens the world Thou hast
    made;
The close coiling chain
That strangles the heart; the burden that weighs
On the wings that would soar.

Lord take away pain from the world Thou hast
    made,
That it loves Thee the more!

Then answered the Lord to the world He had made
    Shall I take away pain;
    And with it the power of the soul to endure,
    Made strong by the strain?
    Shall I take away pity, that knits heart to heart,
    And sacrifice high?
    Will you lose all your heroes that lift from the
        flame
    White brows to the sky?
    Shall I take away love that redeems with a price?
    And smiles through the loss?
    Can ye spare from the lives that would climb
        unto mine
    The Christ on His Cross?

C. L. Drawbridge
(Quoted by Hugh Evan Hopkins in
The Mystery of Suffering)

3 The library

He was despised and rejected by men,
    a man of sorrows and familiar with suffering.
Like one from whom men hide their faces
    he was despised, and we esteemed him not.
Surely he took up our infirmities
    and carried our sorrows,
yet we considered him stricken by God,
    smitten by him, and afflicted.
But he was pierced for our transgressions,
    he was crushed for our iniquities;
the punishment that brought us peace was upon him,
    and by his wounds we are healed.

Isaiah 53: 3–5

Here is one of the many great high points of the Old
Testament. The dawning awareness suddenly comes over

the speaker that this despised human being, passed over in his suffering and total weakness, is the very earthen vessel God is using to bring healing to mankind. The Servant's totally innocent suffering 'brought us peace' (shalom, the nearest Old Testament idea to health and wholeness), and his innocent wounds brought healing to mankind. This is a unique insight in the Old Testament that was to be fulfilled in the New. It was not the strength of God's Servant that would avail to effect such a redemptive healing of cosmic proportions: rather it was his weakness. The fact that 'by his wounds we are healed', is an experience put into words which unfolds a whole new revelation. The path to wholeness cannot be attained solely through our own effort, but through someone called by God to suffer on our behalf. It is by his stripes, not our own.

This fourth Servant Song ends with the words:

> For he bore the sin of many
>   and made intercession for the transgressors. (v.12)

This act of intercession is more than words. It is acted out in deed also, as the Servant offers his very suffering as the act of intercession. Here is the word/deed theme found in the person of Moses and fulfilled in Jesus, the second Moses, picked up by Isaiah and lived out in the person of the Servant in these prophecies. He 'made intercession' by offering his own life, expressive of the true meaning of the word, 'to take up your stance in between God and man'. This work is perfectly fulfilled in the healing ministry and teaching of Jesus, which reached its climax in the deed of innocent suffering on the Cross.

M. M., *Journey to Wholeness*, pp 27f

4 *The music room*

A Memory of Kreisler once:
At some recital in this same city,
The seats all taken, I found myself pushed
On to the stage with a few others,

So near that I could see the toil
Of his face muscles, a pulse like a moth
Fluttering under the fine skin,
And the indelible veins of his smooth brow.

I could see, too, the twitching of the fingers,
Caught temporarily in art's neurosis,
As we sat there or warmly applauded
This player who so beautifully suffered
For each of us upon his instrument.

So it must have been on Calvary
In the fiercer light of the thorn's halo:
The men standing by and that one figure,
The hands bleeding, the mind bruised but calm,
Making such music as lives still.
And no one daring to interrupt
Because it was himself that he played
And closer than all of them the God listened.

R. S. Thomas (1913–   ), *The Musician*

5 *The quiet room*

'By his wounds we are healed' or 'He died that we might be
forgiven' – this has been the Christian tradition of belief.
Father Gerald O'Collins in *The Calvary Christ* has this to say:

> Before Jesus could cause our healing, he had to be
> crucified. His execution prompted the healing. In that
> sense, if uncrucified he would not have been our healer.
> Being made perfect 'through what he suffered,' he could
> become 'the source of eternal salvation to all who obey
> him' (Hebrews 5: 8f). Again, it was the whole Jesus who
> was crucified, not – so to speak – just some part of him.
> Crucifixion destroyed his entire human existence. What
> remained uncrucified in him would be unhealed in us.

*   *   *   *

Jürgen Moltmann in *The Church in the Power of the Spirit*,
says:

> God experiences history in order to effect history. He
> goes out of himself in order to gather into himself. He is

vulnerable, takes suffering and death on himself *in order to heal*, to liberate and to confer new life.

* * * *

Dietrich Bonhoeffer, shortly before his execution, wrote:

Christ helps us, not by virtue of his omnipotence, but by virtue of his weakness and suffering. Only the suffering God can help . . . Man is summoned to share in God's sufferings at the hands of a godless world.

* * * *

Jesus said three times in St Mark's gospel:

The Son of Man must suffer.

* * * *

> Vine of heaven, thy Blood supplies
> This blest cup of sacrifice;
> Lord, thy wounds our healing give;
> To thy cross we look and live;
> Thou our life! O let us be
> Rooted, grafted, built on thee.
>> J. Conder (1789–1855)

6 *The living room*

We bring our work to your working hands,
We bring our sickness to your healing hands,
We bring our weakness to your strong hands,
We bring our sadness to your tender hands,
We bring our needs to your praying hands,
We bring our suffering to your wounded hands,
We bring our love, our families and our children to
    your hands outstretched to bless,
We bring our hands to share with you that bread of
    love we take from you,
That we may take your sacramental presence to
    share with others.
As we take your hands,

we are to be those hands in the world
today. Amen.
C. I. Pettit in a service for Good Friday

Lord, use my hands; they are not scarred like
thine;
They have not felt the torture of the cross:
But they would know upon their palms
Thy touch, without which all their work is loss.

Lord, use my hands, that some may see, not me,
But thy divine compassion there expressed,
And know thy peace, and feel thy calm and rest.
A Fijian nurse's prayer

Father, we bring to you the needs of those whose lives are
shadowed by suffering, praying especially for those
whose sickness has no known cure, whose sadness finds
no comfort, and whose loneliness can never be filled.
Bind up their wounds, O Lord, in the healing wounds of
your Son, and lift their hearts to you as now in silence we
remember them in his holy name of Jesus, Saviour and
Healer. Amen.
NPP 300, adapted

7 The door into the world

Now I rejoice in what was suffered for you, and I fill up in
my flesh what is still lacking in regard to Christ's afflic-
tions, for the sake of his body, which is the church.
Colossians 1: 24

Suffering is the very best gift he has to give us. He gives it
only to his chosen friends.
St Thérèse of Lisieux

When one is in very great pain and fear it is extremely
difficult to pray coherently, and I could only raise my
mind in anguish to God and ask for strength to hold on.
Dr Sheila Cassidy

Ask God to give thee skill
   In comfort's art;
That thou mayst consecrated be
   And set apart,
Into a life of sympathy.
For heavy is the weight of ill
   In every heart;
And comforters are needed much
   Of Christlike touch.

A. E. Hamilton
(Elizabeth Basset, *Love is My Meaning*,
Darton, Longman & Todd 1973)

Lord, use my hands, that some may see, not me,
   But thy divine compassion there expressed,
And know thy peace, and feel thy calm and
      rest.   Amen.

And the God of all grace, who called you to his eternal
glory in Christ, after you have suffered a little while, will
himself restore you and make you strong, firm and
steadfast. To him be the power for ever and ever.
Amen.

1 Peter 5: 10, 11

DAY 7

CALLED TO CARE AND HEAL

1 *The entrance to the house of God's glory*

The vocation of every man and woman is to serve other people.

Count Leo Tolstoy

One of those days Jesus went out into the hills to pray, and spent the night praying to God. When morning came, he called his disciples to him and chose twelve of them, whom he also designated apostles . . . When Jesus had called the Twelve together, he gave them power and authority to drive out all demons and to cure diseases, and he sent them out to preach the kingdom of God and to heal the sick.

Luke 6: 12, 13; 9: 1, 2

Lord Jesus, who chose twelve disciples and sent them forth to preach the gospel and to heal the sick: Forgive the faithless disobedience of thy children, and help us to restore the healing ministry to thy Church. Grant that thy whole Church as thy body may be inspired to teach and to heal; that again signs may follow upon faith in thee, and the world may know that thou art our mighty Saviour; to whom be all praise and glory, now and for evermore.   Amen.

Guild of Health

2 *The therapy room*

O MOST MERCIFUL,
>   hear my prayer for grace
>   to be a good workman in thy kingdom;
and when thou hearest,
>   forgive.

Work in me of thy good pleasure
>   both to will and to do thy work,
>   the work thou willest, when thou willest,
>   as thou willest;
– thine own incessant work
>   of truth, sympathy, healing, joy;
work that speaks, none knows how, nor I,
>   the tongue of heaven;
>   and reveals thyself.

Thou, O God, art in love with all thy work;
>   it flows, it pours, out of thy heart.
In the bounty of thy grace
>   make me, O Father, an instrument of it;
the thought be thine, the word thine, the deed
>   thine,
>   the glory all thine:
enough for me
>   the obedience.   Amen.

>   Eric Milner-White, *My God, My Glory,*
>   SPCK 1954, 111

3 *The library*

What is pastoral care? Two Americans, with the unlikely
names of Clebsch and Jaekle, in *Pastoral Care in Historical
Perspective* . . . define pastoral care as 'Helping acts, done
by representative Christian persons, directed towards
the *healing, sustaining, guiding* and *reconciling* of troubled
persons whose troubles arise in the context of ultimate
meanings and concerns . . .' 'It is exercised at a depth
where the meaning of life and faith is involved on the part
of the helper as well as on the part of the one helped.'
Pastoral care, that is, will be exercised by a Christian in
accordance with what he believes about the nature and

destiny of man, and . . . the motivation for pastoral care in the first place derives from what he believes not only about man, but also about the eternal nature of God. That will not mean that he will inflict that meaning on others, even if he will always be ready to 'give a reason for the hope that is in him.' It will mean that he will never give up the search for greater clarity, greater depth of understanding of persons and their relationships with each other and with God. He will, that is, always be a student in a life-long educational process.

So to *healing* . . . To be a *healer* (in this sense) is to recognise and understand something of the source of another person's wounds. It isn't to be in the analysis-business, or to pretend to a professionalism which is superfluous. It isn't, either, so to concentrate on the wound that the wound becomes the person and its healer sees a problem and not a person. It is to give the wound space, time, air; it isn't to be ready to apply a miracle cure, or a magical adhesive plaster, or to take away the risk of scars. It is to allow the poison to seep out, and in so doing to be ready to absorb it. If bitterness has been allowed to drain away, scars can be valuable evidence of suffering experienced and transformed. Some wounds are of such long-standing, have cut so deep, that the poison has already done its lasting work; the job of the healer then becomes the job of the guider. Sometimes the wounds are hard to get at, because to avoid the hurt they cause us, we have pushed them hard away, though they were too painful even to examine; we've found the memory too keen, or the guilt too hard to bear. But trying to forget, trying to act as though they never were, only makes wounds more poisonous still. And the task of the healer we're called to be is gently to help the other to recognise the hidden sore.

There is no trick by which this can be done. It may be that sometimes, and where appropriate, we can help the other person to put his wounds in the context of Christ's wounds, linking our little pains with the great suffering of God in Christ. That will not take the pain away; but it will make it more bearable. Chiefly, and not surprisingly, it will be our own *selves*, our presence, which will be the healing resource, and the more open our presence is to

God, the greater our intimacy with him, the greater the
confidence, the greater the chance of liberation we shall
encourage.

Perhaps, then, to be an *agent* of healing is a more apt
phrase to us than 'healer', since it points to the origin and
fount of all healing.

Frank Wright, *Pastoral Care for Lay People*, pp 23–5,
SCM Press 1982

4 The music room

Now let us from this table rise,
    renewed in body, mind, and soul;
With Christ we die and live again,
    his selfless love has made us whole.

With minds alert, upheld by grace,
    to spread the Word in speech and deed,
We follow in the steps of Christ,
    at one with man in hope and need.

To fill each human house with love,
    it is the sacrament of care;
The work that Christ began to do
    we humbly pledge ourselves to share.

Then give us courage, Father God,
    to choose again the pilgrim way,
And help us to accept with joy
    the challenge of tomorrow's day.

Fred Kaan (1929–), HFT 70

Lord, as I repeat, slowly, those words of the third verse, I
offer them to you as my act of personal re-dedication.
Accept my pledge, for your holy name's sake. Amen.

5 The quiet room

Healing – Sustaining – Guiding – Reconciling – the words we
were given in *the library* today to describe a caring ministry.
We see this caring in the action of the Good Samaritan.

Read Luke 10: 25–37

The Samaritan's immediate reaction was to stop, to allow his journey for the time being to become of secondary importance and to place himself at the disposal of the wounded traveller – an act of compassion, a willingness to suffer along with him.

Healing the wounds – the first need. Oil, a natural emollient with healing properties; wine, an excellent if primitive disinfectant. Both have become outward signs of the Church's healing sacraments, signs of an inward spiritual grace, for so often the wounds we are called upon to help in healing are deeper, inner wounds and hurts, which can be healed by Jesus only.

Sustaining the person – the second need. The Samaritan stayed with the traveller, actually taking full responsibility for his welfare – for a time, until he could hand him over to someone he trusted. We too may have to stay with a fellow traveller – for just as long as we are needed, but no longer.

Guiding along the true way – the third need. The Samaritan's purpose was to guide the traveller back on to the journey of his true destiny. He took him to a haven from where, when fully recovered, he could return to his own journey of life.

Reconciling man to man and man to God – the fourth need. The Samaritan saw to it that relationships would also be healed. He had made a tiny contribution towards the healing of the nations by coming to the aid of a wounded Jew. As a traveller the latter would be able to trust his fellow human beings again. The innkeeper, to whom an offering was made, would feel no resentment at having to care for a situation for which he had not been responsible.

Some have seen Jesus in the person of the Good Samaritan. So perhaps HE was taking fallen humanity into the safekeeping of HIS heavenly Father for which HE paid the price of the Cross, and effected the reconciliation of man to God. See 2 Corinthians 5: 18ff. Above all, HE *heals, sustains, guides, reconciles* us, the wounded travellers on life's journey.

* * * *

Some have also seen Jesus in the person of the wounded traveller. When we *heal, sustain, guide, reconcile*, we are privileged to do it for HIM, in the persons of those we help.

I tell you the truth, whatever you did for one of the least
of these brothers of mine, you did for me.

> Matthew 25: 40

*   *   *   *

Lord, teach us to care as you cared,
    empower us to heal as you healed,
and may we do it always to your glory
    for you are both Priest and Victim,
      the Anointing and the Anointed One,
        Jesus Christ, our Healer and Saviour.

> Amen.

6 *The living room*

Lord Jesus, in your days in the body in Palestine you chose
your men that you might send them out to do your work.
We know that you are still looking for hands and voices and
minds to use, and we ask you to bless those whom you are
still sending out on your service.

Bless the ministers of your Church in all its branches.
Make them diligent in study, faithful in pastoral duty,
wise in teaching, fearless and winsome in preaching,
and ever clothed with your grace and love.
Bless those who teach the young in schools, and colleges,
and universities. Make them to think adventurously
and to teach enthusiastically, that they may kindle
and inspire young minds in the search for truth. Help
them to be such that they may infect others with the
contagion of the love of learning, dedicated to the
service of mankind.
Bless those who heal and tend the sick, doctors, surgeons
and nurses. Give them skill, gentleness and sympathy,
so that, when it is possible to heal, they may do so,
and, when it is not possible, they may bring help and
comfort to those who enter into the valley of the
shadow.
Bless fathers and mothers to whom you have committed
the trust of a little child. Help them to build a home in
which wise discipline and understanding walk hand in
hand.

Bless those who do the world's work, and grant that whatever they do they may do for you, so that they may never offer less than their best, and so that they may be workmen who have no need to be ashamed.

So grant that all your servants, faithfully serving you and their fellow men, may prepare themselves and those amongst whom they work for your coming again. This we ask for your love's sake.   Amen.

William Barclay, *Prayers for the Christian Year*, SCM Press 1964

7 *The door into the world*

Only the Holy Spirit can safely direct our healing power. And if we will listen to the voice of God within, we will be shown for whom to pray.   Agnes Sanford

> God of love, giver of life and health,
>   we pray for all who in their various callings
> serve the needs of men and women
>   in sickness of body, mind or spirit.
> Equip them as your fellow workers
>   in the ministry of healing,
> and strengthen them to share in the task
>   of making life whole;
> through Jesus Christ our Lord.   Amen.
>   Basil Naylor, CPP 434

A nurse's prayer
  Lord Jesus, teach us to see the patients through
    your eyes,
      and may they feel your touch through our
      hands;
  so that we shall prepare to welcome you in our
    hearts,
      and truly know your healing and
      peace.   Amen.
                        Cicely Small

  Lord, go with us this day
    as we seek to answer your calls
      to care and heal.   Amen.

DAY 8

CELEBRATE THE PRESENT MOMENT

1 *The entrance to the house of God's glory*

> Come, let us sing for joy to the Lord;
>   let us shout aloud to the Rock of our salvation.
> Let us come before him with thanksgiving
>   and extol him with music and song . . .
> Come, let us bow down in worship,
>   let us kneel before the Lord our Maker;
> for he is our God and we are the people of his
>   pasture,
>   the flock under his care.
> TODAY, if you hear his voice,
>   do not harden your hearts . . .
>
> Psalm 95: 1, 2, 6, 7, 8

Throughout the course of your daily life make use of the opportunities offered you to take a new hold on yourself and to welcome God into your life: while you're waiting for the bus, or for your motor to warm up, or for your supper to cook, or for the milk to boil, or for your coffee to cool off, or for a free telephone booth, or for the traffic lights to change . . . Don't *kill time*; no matter how short it is, it can be *a moment of grace*. The Lord is there, and he is inviting you to reflection and decision so that you can become a human being in the fullest sense.

Michel Quoist, The Christian Response, p 75,
Gill and Son, Dublin 1975

May we accept this day at your hand, O God,
   as a gift to be treasured,

a life to be enjoyed,
a trust to be kept,
and a hope to be fulfilled;
and all for your glory.   Amen.

Stanley Pritchard, NPP 530

2 *The therapy room*

Forgive, and you will be forgiven.

Luke 6: 37

Bishop Festo Kivengere had an argument with his wife
one evening. Afterwards he had to go out and preach, so
he said goodbye and went off. But as he walked down the
drive, God spoke to him – and this is how Bishop Festo
described the ensuing dialogue between himself and his
Lord.

'Festo,' said the Lord, 'you go back and apologise to
your wife.'

'But Lord, I've got a very important sermon to preach.'

'You go and apologise to your wife.'

'But Lord, there are hundreds of people waiting for me
and we're going to have a good time tonight.'

'You go and apologise to your wife.'

'But Lord, I'm almost late and someone's waiting to
collect me.'

'All right', the Lord said, 'you go and preach your
sermon and I'm going to stay with your wife in the
kitchen.'

Bishop Festo ended the story with these words: 'I went
back into the kitchen and apologised. So there was
revival in the kitchen before there was revival in the
church.'

Through the Year with David Watson, January 14,
Hodder 1982

Let us use the sacrament of this present moment to seek
forgiveness from the Lord by forgiving anyone with whom
we are at variance, or resolving to seek their forgiveness.

Lord, in this moment and in your presence,
I pray for your love for . . .

Take all hurt, resentment, ill feeling away from our
    relationship,
And grant us both to experience your forgiveness
    and healing,
        now, and for ever.   Amen.

TODAY, if you hear his voice,
    do not harden your hearts.

Psalm 95: 8

Forgiveness and celebration are at the heart of
community.

Jean Vanier

3 *The library*

The sacrament of the present moment

God uses his creatures in two ways. Either he makes
them act on their own initiative or he himself acts
through them. The first requires a faithful fulfilment of
his manifest wishes; the second, a meek and humble
submission to his inspiration. Surrender of self achieves
them both, being nothing more than a total commitment
to the word of God *within the present moment*. It is not
important for his creatures to know how they must do
this or what the nature of the present moment is. What
is absolutely essential is an unreserved surrender of
themselves.

A contrite and submissive heart opens the way to
pleasing God. An ecstasy of perfect love pervades the
fulfilment of his will by those who surrender to it; and
this surrender practised each moment embodies every
kind of virtue and excellence. It is not for us to determine
what manner of submission we owe to God, but only
humbly to submit to and be ready to accept everything
that comes to us. The rest is up to him . . .

Living in God in this way the heart is dead to all else
and all else is dead to it. For it is God alone who gives life
to all things, who quickens the soul in the creature and
the creature in the soul. God's word is that life. With it the
heart and the creature are one. Without it they are

strangers. Without the virtue of the divine will all creation is reduced to nothing; with it, it is brought into the realm of his kingdom where every moment is complete contentment in God Alone, and a total surrender of all creatures to his order. *It is the sacrament of the present moment.*

Jean-Pierre de Caussade, S.J., *The Sacrament of the Present Moment*, Fount paperbacks 1981 (First published in France as *L'Abandon à la Providence divine*, 1966)

4 *The music room*

Praise to the Lord, the Almighty, the King of
    creation;
O my soul, praise him, for he is thy health and
    salvation:
Come ye who hear,
Brothers and sisters draw near,
Praise him in glad adoration.

Praise to the Lord, who o'er all things so
    wondrously reigneth,
Shelters thee under his wings, yea, so gently
    sustaineth:
Hast thou not seen
All that is needful hath been
Granted in what he ordaineth?

Praise to the Lord, who doth prosper thy work,
    and defend thee;
Surely his goodness and mercy here daily attend
    thee:
Ponder anew
All the Almighty can do,
He who with love doth befriend thee.

Praise to the Lord, who when sickness with terror
    uniting,
Deaf to entreaties of mortals, its victims is smiting,
Pestilence quells,
Sickness and fever dispels,
Grateful thanksgiving inviting.

Praise to the Lord! O let all that is in me adore him!
All that hath life and breath come now with praises
    before him!
Let the amen
Sound from his people again:
Gladly for ay we adore him.

J. Neander (1650–80), EH 536

At the heart of celebration, there are the poor. If the least significant is excluded, it is no longer a celebration . . . A celebration must always be a festival of the poor.

Jean Vanier, Community and Growth, p 235, Darton,
Longman & Todd 1979

5 *The quiet room*

'Celebrate the moment with God'

Without looking back, you want to follow Christ: here and now, *in the present moment, turn to God* and trust in the Gospel. In so doing, you draw from the sources of jubilation.

You think you do not know how to pray. Yet the risen Christ is there; he loves you before you love him. By 'his Spirit who dwells in your hearts', he intercedes in you far more than you imagine.

Even without recognising him, learn to wait for him with or without words, during long silences when nothing seems to happen. There obsessive discouragements vanish, creative impulses well up. Nothing can be built up in you without this adventure – finding him in the intimacy of a personal encounter. No one can do it for you.

When you have trouble understanding what he wants of you, tell him so. In the course of daily activities, *at every moment, tell him all*, even things you cannot bear.

Do not compare yourself with others, and with what they can do. Why wear yourself out regretting what is impossible for you? Could you have forgotten God? Turn to him. No matter what happens, dare to begin over and over again.

If you were to accuse yourself of all that is in you, your

days and nights would not suffice. You have something better to do; *in the present moment, celebrate God's forgiveness*, despite the resistances of believing yourself forgiven, whether by God or by others.

When inner trials or incomprehensions from without make themselves felt, remember that in the very same wound where the poison of anxiety festers, there too the energies for loving are born.

If you seem to be walking in a thick fog, waiting for him, Christ, means giving him the time to put everything in its place . . . A fountain of gladness will spring up in the desert of your heart. Not a euphoric bliss, not just any kind of joy, but that jubilation which comes straight from the wellsprings of Eternity.

Brother Roger of Taizé, *Parable of Community*, Mowbray 1980

6 *The living room*

This is a critical moment in world history, a moment when God is asking us whether we really intend to deal honestly with him. It is an hour when God is bringing the world to an awareness of how far short its love and faith really fall. It is an hour when God's demand is falling upon us, an hour in which we have to make a decision. One path leads to a mankind without God, to a human freedom which does not know itself to be dependent on anything – not even on love, faith, and values. The other path leads to a realization of all the things that are worthwhile in life, to a recognition of the reality of conscience, obligation, and responsibility. To an acknowledgement of God. This is an hour when all mankind must decide.

Franz Cardinal König, *The Hour is Now*,
Gill & Macmillan 1975

Let us pause in this moment of prayer –

*   *   *   *

First, to bring before God, one by one, the main items of news carried by the newspapers and television bulletins at this time.

Let us be aware 'of how far short love and faith really fall'.

LORD, HAVE MERCY.

Then, let us imagine ourselves in that situation confronted
by the two paths:
> one towards 'mankind without God';
> the other towards 'an acknowledgement of
> God' and
>   'all the things that are worthwhile in life'.

It is 'the hour in which we have to make a decision'.
> LORD, GUIDE US.

*   *   *   *

We pray as fellow members of the human race, that the
people involved in each situation will take the path of
healing and reconciliation – that is towards GOD, towards
'obligation and responsibility', towards 'love, faith and
values.'
> LORD, HEAR US.   Amen.

7 The door into the world

Let no debt remain outstanding, except the continuing
debt to love one another, for he who loves his fellow man
has fulfilled the law . . .

And do this, *understanding the present time*. The hour has
come for you to wake up from your slumber, because our
salvation is nearer now than when we first believed. The
night is nearly over, the day is almost here. So let us put
aside the deeds of darkness and put on the armour of
light.

Romans 13: 8, 11, 12

> Give us grace, O Lord, to live each day
> > as if it were the day of your coming.
>
> May we be urgent to prepare your way
> > by fighting all evil,
> > by preaching the gospel,
> > by feeding the hungry,
> > by releasing the oppressed,
> > and by healing the sick.
>
> So may we hasten the triumph of your kingdom,
> > and bring glory to your name.   Amen.
> > > John Kingsnorth, NPP 70

Maranatha: even so come, Lord Jesus.   Amen.

DAY 9

CHRISTIANITY AND MEDICINE

1 *The entrance to the house of God's glory*

Praise the Lord, O my soul.
   I will praise the Lord all my life;
   I will sing praise to my God as long as I live.
He upholds the cause of the oppressed
   and gives food to the hungry.
The Lord sets prisoners free,
   the Lord gives sight to the blind,
the Lord lifts up those who are bowed down,
   the Lord loves the righteous.
The Lord watches over the alien
   and sustains the fatherless and the widow.
The Lord reigns for ever . . . Praise the Lord.
                              Psalm 146: 1, 2, 7–10

Eternal Lord God,
   as is your majesty, so is your mercy.
Open our eyes to your light,
   our hearts to your love,
   and our minds to your truth,
that we may praise you now and always,
      through Jesus Christ our Lord.   Amen.
                    New Every Morning, BBC, p 71

Sanctify, O Lord, those whom you have called to the
study and practice of the arts of healing, and to the
prevention of disease and pain. Strengthen them by your
life-giving Spirit, that by their ministries the health of

the community may be promoted and your creation glorified; through Jesus Christ our Lord.   Amen.

Episcopal Church of the USA, NPP 277

2 *The therapy room*

Heal Us Together to Work

Lord Jesus Christ, you came to make us whole,
    a whole person, a whole society, a whole people.
Yet our wrong thinking has led to false action,
    our misguided individualism to disintegration,
    our selfishness to a lack of community;
        have mercy upon us and forgive us.
We have dissipated your healing power,
    by dividing the whole person you created,
    separating the care for the body from the care of
      the mind,
      and both from the care of the soul;
erecting walls of partition between those who
      engage in therapy,
    between the different medical disciplines,
    between them and alternative therapists,
    between all and the churches, –
        even between the churches themselves;
      have mercy upon us and forgive us.

May we learn from you and again appropriate your healing power, bringing all who seek to heal the sick into a unity
      of mind and will within your healing
        community;
Lord of all therapy and therapists,
    HEAL US TOGETHER TO WORK
in your name.   Amen.

3 *The library*

Few serious modern Christian theologians would lightly reject the theological reasoning of St Basil or his close friend, Gregory of Nazianzus, yet these men also wrote of Christian healing. Is there any sound reason to ignore their thinking on the subject? Both had a good knowledge of medicine for their time – Basil, indeed, had some medical training – and with health none too good, both had a direct interest in practical medicine. Gregory also had reason to be aware of the brilliant medical career of his brother Caesarius, while Basil founded and maintained a large hospital outside Caesarea – probably the first public institution devoted to care of the sick. At the same time, the two men were equally committed to the reality of healing through Christ. In place after place Gregory showed his understanding of the 'deep roots' of disease and how closely the church's task with people was allied to the job of the medical practitioner . . .

Gregory recounts some remarkable healings in his immediate family. One instance was widely known locally. His sister Gorgonia was dragged by a team of mules and so frightfully injured that no one thought she could recover; she was saved by the prayers of the congregation. Years later she had a second experience, which was understandably not spoken of outside the family while she lived. Gregory describes her illness as a burning fever alternating with periods of deathlike coma, with only brief remissions. He recounts how it continued in spite of prayers and all that several physicians could do. One night, in the middle of the night, she somehow made her way into the church and in despair took some of the reserved sacrament in her hand and knelt, grasping the altar. Crying out that she would hold on until she was made whole, she rubbed the precious substance on her body, and at last stood up, refreshed and stronger; she knew she was saved, and again a miraculous recovery had begun.

Several other events of this kind appear in Gregory's writings, and in his theological poems the healing miracles of the Bible are made vividly alive. This fascinating family was so deeply at home in the reality of the spiritual world that healing could be sought and received naturally as a gift from God. It is no wonder that Gregory of Nazianzus was in so many ways the pivot on whom the establishment of an orthodox faith depended.

St Basil was interested in practical matters and therefore in healing. In *The Long Rules*, one of the important treatises on monastic life, he considered the question of 'whether recourse to the medical art is in keeping with the practice of piety.' His thinking has a modern ring to it. Medical science has been given to men by God, he contended, to be used when necessary, although not as the only decisive factor. Just as the Lord sometimes healed merely by uttering a command and sometimes by physical touch, so 'He sometimes cures us secretly and without visible means when He judges this mode of treatment beneficial to our souls; and again He wills that we use material remedies for our ills.'

He discussed the various natural remedies provided by medicine, implying that these are also gifts for which God is to be thanked, and remarking that 'to reject entirely the benefits to be derived from this art is the sign of a petty nature.' On the other hand, there were reasons why a man might suffer sickness or fail to be healed. In considering them Basil did not deny either kind of healing to anyone, except possibly a saint like Paul. It might be necessary, he said, for a saint to suffer some infirmity to know that he was human, but 'those who have contracted illness by living improperly should make use of the healing of their body as a type and exemplar, so to speak, for the cure of their soul.'

In other words, saints and sinners alike might expect to suffer for getting off the beam, but redemption – for sinners at least – was very much like the healing of physical illness. The expectation of healing as a normal Christian phenomenon apparently continued throughout Basil's active life.

Morton T. Kelsey, *Healing and Christianity*, SCM Press 1973

4 *The music room*

O God, whose will is life and good
    for all of mortal breath,
Unite in bonds of brotherhood
    all those who fight with death.

Make strong their hands and hearts and wills
   to drive disease afar,
To battle with the body's ills,
   and wage thy holy war.

Where'er they heal the sick and blind,
   Christ's love may they proclaim;
Make known the good Physician's mind,
   and prove the Saviour's name.

Before them set thy holy will,
   that they, with heart and soul,
To thee may consecrate their skill,
   and make the sufferer whole.

                H. D. Rawnsley (1851–1920), HFT 75

5 The quiet room

With the re-emergence of the idea of wholeness in Christianity, rooted in the Godhead itself, and with the re-
emergence in science of a wholistic view of the universe,
perhaps the foundations of this new fiduciary framework
are already being laid. This is significant for the coming
together of Medicine and Christianity, especially when
applied to the concept of health. For the term 'wholeness'
becomes increasingly meaningful for both since it is
descriptive not only of the unity of the personality, but
also of the healing process itself. It is this concept of
wholeness that holds out the greatest hope for the coming together of the healing professions. And even though
not all in medicine will acknowledge the contribution
that Christianity has to make, the vast majority would
acknowledge that a sense of purpose or a meaningful
orientation is necessary to the wholeness of a person,
indeed to life itself. Christians would think of this as the
spiritual factor and would see spiritual therapy as the
vital contribution they would be able to offer. The most
health-giving, wholistic and meaningful orientation that
can be offered in the Christian view is a relationship with
God, the source of all wholeness. That relationship is
incarnated in the person of Jesus Christ, and Christians
see him as the norm for what it means to be whole as well

as the source of wholeness in the lives of those who accept him as Lord, Saviour and Healer. It is this kind of 'other' relationship to which Carl Jung referred when he stated he could heal no one without first restoring to them their religious sense. The person who has an-other dimension to their life, in particular that relationship with the Christ who heals, has a head start on the journey to wholeness. The fact that this is gaining acceptance in medical circles may well provide the framework within which can be constructed a new partnership between the Church and Medicine in the caring for people with which both are entrusted.

M.M., *Journey to Wholeness*, SPCK 1986, pp 82 f

*　*　*　*

Do I recognise Jesus Christ as the source of wholeness in my life?

*　*　*　*

Is Jesus Christ my Lord, Saviour and Healer?

*　*　*　*

Lord Jesus, in these times of quiet, may my life draw nearer to yours, in every way, and so find healing.　Amen.

6 *The living room*

It is the dimension of prayer and the exercise of the sovereignly distributed Holy Spirit gifts given for the occasion that enables healing to occur in ways and at levels quite inaccessible to secular therapies. Many of these can uncover past wounds, unravel complexes and accurately discern the inner plight of people, but none known to me has the power to undo the past, to transform the tangled web woven deep in a person's history and to remake an injured personality – in short, to redeem the person. To pretend that they can is presumptuous, but to discard them because of their limitations is surely equally unreasonable.

I believe we need to work for a truly functioning

partnership of all that modern medical practice has to offer, utilising sound psychological principles and working with the rich, though often neglected, resources of the Church. Healing is not the exclusive domain of either medicine or the Church, rather it is a joint task in which both disciplines complement each other.

> Dr Ruth Fowke, *We Believe in Healing*, edited by
> Dr Ann England, Highland Books

Let us pray for the joint ministry of the Church and Medicine:

Heavenly Father, we know that all healing comes from you, and therefore we ask your blessing on all who are engaged in the ministry of healing.
 We pray for doctors, surgeons and psychiatrists,
 for health visitors and district nurses,
 for chaplains and intercessors,
 for the staff who work in our local hospitals,
 for our parish priest(s) and for our own doctor,
 and for those who nurse the sick at home.
 Give them, O Lord, all needful wisdom, skill and
  patience;
and may they know that in ministering to the sick they are fellow workers with you and are furthering your purposes of love; through Jesus Christ our Lord. Amen.

> Adapted NPP 280

7 The door into the world

Both Medicine and Church are being called to leave their ivory towers and to adopt a more outgoing, missionary, community concept of care.

> Dr Bob Lambourne, *Health Today and Salvation Today*,
> Birmingham University 1983

Lord, teach us not to cling to our vested interests,
  hiding behind the curtain of dogma and
  tradition.
Rather make us adventurous,

willing to leave our tightly-held corner.
Give us a wholeness and largeness of view
   as you demonstrated in your ministry,
   Totally outgoing, for it is the world you came to
     save
      and we are now your hands;
   Totally missionary, for it is you who sent us
    about our business
      and we are now your feet;
   Totally united in community, for both Church
and Medicine
      are the instruments of your healing
      showing forth your compassionate heart.
Teach us to care as you cared,
   and send us, your healing community, to
     preach and heal,
so that your people may turn to you
   and know you to be their health and salvation,
     even Jesus Christ our Lord.   Amen.

To him who loves us and has freed us from our sins by his
blood, and has made us to be a kingdom and priests to
serve his God and Father – to him be glory and power for
ever and ever.   Amen.

                             Revelation 1: 5, 6

DAY 10

COMPASSION

1 *The entrance to the house of God's glory*

Great crowds came to (Jesus), bringing the lame, the
blind, the crippled, the dumb and many others, and laid
them at his feet; and he healed them. The people were
amazed when they saw the dumb speaking, the crippled
made well, the lame walking and the blind seeing. And
they praised the God of Israel.

Jesus called his disciples to him and said, '*I have compassion for these people . . .*'

Matthew 15: 30–32

Jesus knew what was in man, and his attitude toward
men who were caught in moral, mental, or physical
illness was one of compassion. He was able to respond
freely and directly because he knew that there were
causes of sickness and suffering beyond human control.
Nowhere in the Gospels is there any suggestion of Jesus
asking a sick person what he had done or whether he had
sinned before healing him. Instead he took direct action
to meet the need. Even the healing of the Gentile child,
the daughter of the Canaanite (or Syrophoenician)
woman in Matthew 15: 22–28, was given freely and
without any strings attached.

Morton T. Kelsey, *Healing and Christianity*, p 65,
SCM Press 1973

Lord Jesus Christ, who in the days of your life here on
earth showed compassion to the sick and afflicted and
made them whole: bless all of us who seek to carry on

your healing work today. Give us sympathy and skill, a
like compassion and knowledge of your presence; that in
your mercy and to your glory those who suffer in body,
mind or spirit may be restored to fullness of health. We
ask it in the power of your holy name.   Amen.

Adapted from a prayer by Frank Colquhoun, CPP 437

2 *The therapy room*

Compassion in the care for humanity, integrity in the
service of truth, contemplation of God in the stillness of
prayer – may God give these gifts to his Church and to
every one of its members. Serve humanity, reverence
truth, contemplate your Creator.

Michael Ramsey, Archbishop of Canterbury,
in a sermon preached to the University of Cambridge,
February 23rd, 1964.

Today we examine ourselves about
      our compassion and care for others;
      in what spirit do we serve our fellow human
      beings?
            LORD, HAVE MERCY

*   *   *   *

We examine ourselves concerning our integrity in
   the service
      of truth; do we reverence truth?
      Jesus said, I am the truth.
            CHRIST, HAVE MERCY

*   *   *   *

We examine ourselves about our prayer –
      how frequently, how devotedly, do we seek
      out
      a stillness that we may contemplate our
      Creator?
            LORD, HAVE MERCY

OUR FATHER . . .

3 *The library*

The Compassionate God

There is a crucial need for a return to the vision of the God revealed in and by Jesus Christ, the tender, loving and compassionate God who raises men up and makes them whole wherever they have been cast down by the world of evil – whether they have sinned and need forgiveness, or are sick and need physical healing. Even now the kingdom of God is among us, saving and healing and destroying the kingdom of evil.

In short, the nature of God as manifested visibly in Jesus Christ is love. Jesus' compassion impelled him to reach out whenever he saw a sick man, even when it was against his own best interests. (When he cured on the Sabbath, far from proving anything, it showed many of his contemporaries that he was *not* the Messiah.) The healing works of Jesus were so important in Peter's mind that when he gave the household of Cornelius a thumb-nail sketch of the life of Jesus, he said nothing about the content of his preaching, but only reported:

> I take it you know what has been reported all over Judea about Jesus of Nazareth, beginning in Galilee with the baptism John preached; of the way God anointed him *with the Holy Spirit and power*. He went about *doing good works and healing all who were in the grip of the devil*, and God was with him. We are witnesses *to all that he did* in the land of the Jews and in Jerusalem. Acts 10: 37–39, italics added.

After this, Peter speaks of Jesus' crucifixion, death, and resurrection; but he sums up the entire public ministry of Jesus in terms of what he did rather than of what he said, for Jesus established the kingdom of God through the power of healing as well as through preaching.

The healing of Jesus, then, is central to the doctrine of the gospel. To deny this is, in effect, to deny the gospel – to change it from Good News into Good Advice which lacks the power to transform man into a new creation.

Francis MacNutt, *Healing*, p 107 f,
Ave Maria Press, Notre Dame, Indiana 1974

4 *The music room*

> Love divine, all loves excelling,
>> Joy of heaven, to earth come down,
> Fix in us thy humble dwelling,
>> All thy faithful mercies crown.
>
> Jesu, *thou art all compassion,*
>> Pure unbounded love thou art;
> Visit us with thy salvation,
>> Enter every trembling heart.
>
> Come, almighty to deliver,
>> Let us all thy grace receive;
> Suddenly return, and never,
>> Never more thy temples leave.
>
> Thee we would be always blessing,
>> Serve thee as thy hosts above;
> Pray, and praise thee, without ceasing,
>> Glory in thy perfect love.
>
> Finish then thy new creation:
>> Pure and spotless let us be;
> Let us see thy great salvation,
>> Perfectly restored in thee;
>
> Changed from glory into glory,
>> Till in heaven we take our place,
> Till we cast our crowns before thee,
>> Lost in wonder, love, and praise.
>> Charles Wesley (1707–1788)

This beautiful hymn, much beloved at weddings, is a fine prayer for salvation and healing.

5 *The quiet room*

Jesus called his disciples to him and said,

> 'I have compassion for these people . . .
> I do not want to send them away hungry, or they may collapse on the way.'
>> Matthew 15: 32

When Jesus calls his disciples to him, he has something important to say, in this case concerning his compassion. *He suffers-along-with hungry people. He stays with them.* Let us *feel* his intense compassion for them.

* * * *

There are millions in our world who are dying of starvation, while I have plenty to eat. I can not be whole while they starve. They are my brothers and sisters for whom Christ died.

Lord, teach me your compassion.

There are millions in our world who are dying of a deep spiritual hunger. They do not know their Saviour. 'How can they hear without someone preaching to them? And how can they preach unless they are sent?' Romans 10: 14f.

Lord, here am I. Send me.

* * * *

Let us again *feel* his intense compassion for these hungry millions, each one our brother and sister. He does 'not want to send them away hungry, or they may collapse on the way.'

* * * *

Lord, look with the eye of your compassion on all your people; look especially on each person whom I meet today:

stretch out your hand to heal us in our time
together,
that neither of us may go away hungry,
for we shall have met our companion* by the way,
and been fed with the Bread of Life.
And there will be two less hungry people in your
world,
nourished by our compassionate Saviour.   Amen.

---

* Companion literally means someone with whom you eat bread together.

6 *The living room*

O thou, Lord of all mercy, let thy compassion go out to all
whom thou hast made,
   – to those who are sick or in pain,
   – to those who mourn,
   – to the lonely and to those without hope,
   – to all who sin and do not know that thou thyself hast
      come to us in forgiveness,
   – to all who search for meaning in the universe in the
      life of man and have not found the truth in thee.
Let thy mercy hold them, surround them,
      penetrate them, save them,
         so that they be thine for ever.
Increase in me thy mercy, that my small compassion may
ever accompany thine infinite love,
in gratitude for thy mercy to me and in love for those who
through eternity are to be my companions,
sharers in the mercy brought to us by thy Son,
         our Saviour and Redeemer Jesus Christ.   Amen.

> George Appleton, *One Man's Prayers*, 137

Merciful Lord, who sent your disciples to heal the sick, be
with all those who today have the care of those who
suffer. May their hearts be filled with love and compassion, their hands minister with tenderness, and their
minds be filled with the knowledge that in ministering to
the sick they minister to you.   Amen.

> Paddy Palmer

By the bruising of my whole life,
      strengthen me with sympathy for every
         wounded soul,
   and let my prayers be a balm for the wounds of
         thy children,
      that they may be healed,
         O Lord, my God.   Amen.

> Dorothy Kerin

7 *The door into the world*

> The Lord is gracious and compassionate,
>> slow to anger and rich in love.
> The Lord is good to all:
>> he has compassion on all he has made . . .
> My mouth will speak in praise of the
> Lord.
>> Let every creature praise his holy name
>>> for ever and ever.
>>>> Psalm 145: 8, 9, 21

Lord Jesus we ask you to look with compassion upon all who suffer in body, mind or spirit. Give them comfort and confidence in you; set free the addicted, that strengthened by the power of your Spirit they may be restored to fullness of life, and may all those in pain feel the comfort of your love, that they may be soothed by the knowledge of your presence; we ask it in your name. Amen.

SU

Let us go in peace to love and serve the Lord:
> in the name of Christ. Amen.

DAY 11

FORGIVENESS AND RECONCILIATION

1 *The entrance to the house of God's glory*

When you stand praying, if you hold anything against anyone, forgive him, so that your Father in heaven may forgive you your sins.

Mark 11: 25

Therefore if you are offering your gift at the altar and there remember that your brother has something against you, leave the gift there in front of the altar. First go and be reconciled to your brother; then come and offer your gift.

Matthew 5: 23, 24

Reconciliation sounds a large theological term, but it simply means coming to ourselves and arising and going to our Father.

John Oman

Almighty and everlasting God, who art always more ready to hear than we to pray, and art wont to give more than either we desire or deserve: pour down upon us the abundance of thy mercy; forgiving us those things whereof our conscience is afraid, and giving us those good things which we are not worthy to ask, but through the merits and mediation of Jesus Christ, thy Son, our Lord.   Amen.

BCP

2 *The therapy room*

If we confess our sins, he is faithful and just and will forgive us our sins – to re-establish the broken relationship of mutual love as though our sin had never broken it on our side – and purify us – by his endless and patient striving with us – from all unrighteousness. Lord, I confess. Do thou forgive.

1 John 1: 9

Let me realise that that forgiveness is not just the cancelling of a debt or even the bearing of a burden, still less a 'letting off' of all consequence – but the restoration of a relationship so rich and new that I, even I, can lift up my head and look into thy face and, in spite of all the past, say humbly, even to thee, in this moment: 'There is nothing between us.'   Amen.

Leslie Weatherhead, *A Private House of Prayer*, p 137

*   *   *   *

O Lord, remember not only the men and women of good will, but also those of ill will. But do not remember all the sufferings they have inflicted on us; remember the fruits we bought, thanks to this suffering, – our comradeship, our loyalty, our humility, the courage, the generosity, the greatness of heart which has grown out of this; and when they come to judgment, let all the fruits that we have borne be their forgiveness.

This prayer was found written on a piece of wrapping paper in Ravensbruck, the largest of the concentration camps for women, when it was freed at the close of the 1939–45 war.

J. Neville Ward, *Five for Sorrow, Ten for Joy*, Epworth Press

3 *The library*

The first essential for growth is to be brought into a right relationship with God. Having been brought into that right relationship, there is nothing more important than that we should continue in unclouded fellowship with God. If this is to be our experience, we need constantly to enjoy *the forgiving love of God* . . .

The truth is that first to last our unclouded fellowship

and friendship with him depends, not on our worthiness or goodness or success or anything else, but only and wholly on our being forgiven people . . .

The Bible gives us several pictures to help us grasp the fullness of God's forgiveness. 'As far as the east is from the west', 'I've swept away your offences', 'Into the depths of the sea', 'You have put all my sins behind your back'. One of the most wonderful statements is in Hebrews 8: 12, 'I will forgive their wickedness, and will remember their sins no more.' No more! God actually has the power to put out of his memory the sins he has forgiven. This cannot mean less than that he never brings up against us past sin that he has forgiven. The forgiven sin of yesterday need never cloud today's fellowship. When we feel ashamed to ask his forgiveness again for some sin, perhaps some habit which we consider to be sinful that keeps getting us down, someone has suggested that God says, 'What do you mean *again*?' For there is no past score against us! It is only as we accept his repeated forgiveness that we shall maintain that closeness to him which is the one hope of overcoming the sin, of breaking the habit, for *he alone* can set us free. 'But', someone says, 'don't I have to repent, and doesn't that mean that I commit myself not to do the thing again?' Yes, you do have to repent, but repentance does not mean such a commitment. The Lord knows and we know (if we are aware of our own frailty), that we cannot give that assurance. Repentance is basically a change of mind, a change of direction. It means a change from thinking a thing is not wrong to thinking it is wrong; and a change of direction from looking anywhere else, to one of looking only and wholly to him for the forgiveness and power to set free which he alone can give. It includes an intention to seek his way of freedom . . .

A forgiving spirit will find the way to let drop the many errors, mistakes and shortcomings of others which so often build up resentment in close relationships. It is possible for little things to build up such resentment between two people that they reach the point of not speaking to one another. This does in fact all too frequently happen in marriages, church fellowships and in friendships.

If you have a forgiving spirit, the Lord will show you whether you need to talk to the other person about the thing you have resented or whether you should just let it drop. The vital thing is that we should not let resentment grow by nursing or feeding it. Bring it quickly up into the light of God's presence, talk to him about it and then it will never eat its way into your personality – he will handle it . . .

The more we live in the enjoyment of the wonder and reality of God's forgiving love and his continuous forgiveness, the more will we become forgiving people. The more our hearts are open to his forgiving love, the more our relationships will contribute to our own growth and that of others, because they are free from the destructive factors of guilt, resentment and remorse.

Dr Marion Ashton, *Growing into Wholeness*,
pp 31ff, Kingsway Publications 1985

4 *The music room*

> Christ the Lord is risen again!
> Christ hath broken every chain!
> Hark! angelic voices cry,
> Singing evermore on high,
> > Alleluia!
>
> He who bore all pain and loss
> Comfortless upon the Cross,
> Lives in glory now on high,
> Pleads for us, and hears our cry:
> > Alleluia!
>
> He who slumbered in the grave
> Is exalted now to save;
> Now through Christendom it rings
> That the Lamb is King of Kings,
> > Alleluia!
>
> Now he bids us tell abroad
> How the lost may be restored,
> How the penitent forgiven,
> How we too may enter heaven.
> > Alleluia!

Thou, our Paschal Lamb indeed,
Christ, thy ransomed people feed;
Take our sins and guilt away:
Let us sing by night and day
Alleluia!
M. Weisse, Translated Catherine Winkworth, AMR 136

5 The quiet room

Therefore, if anyone is in Christ, he is a new creation; the
old has gone, the new has come! All this is from God,
who reconciled us to himself through Christ and gave us
the ministry of reconciliation: that God was reconciling
the world to himself in Christ, not counting men's sins
against them. And he has committed to us the message of
reconciliation. We are therefore Christ's ambassadors, as
though God were making his appeal through us – we
implore you on Christ's behalf: *Be reconciled to God*.
2 Corinthians 5: 17–20

*   *   *   *

A love of reconciliation is not weakness or cowardice. It
demands courage, nobility, generosity, sometimes heroism, an overcoming of oneself rather than of one's adver-
sary. At times it may even seem like dishonour, but it
never offends against true justice or denies the rights of
the poor. In reality, it is the patient, wise art of peace, of
loving, of living with one's fellows, after the example
of Christ, with a strength of heart and mind modelled
on his.

Pope Paul VI

*   *   *   *

Lord Christ, who by your cross and passion
    reconciled the world to God
and broke down the barriers of race and colour
    which divide men and nations:
make us and all your people
    instruments of reconciliation in the life of our world,
that we may inherit the blessing
    which you promised to the peacemakers.   Amen.
New Every Morning, p 86, BBC

6 The living room

R. N. Flew wrote that God's forgiveness implies *a personal relationship, violated and now restored.* He also wrote: *Forgiveness means the reception of the sinner into a personal relationship with God: and means too, that this relationship is richer than it was before the relationship had been broken.*

Vincent Taylor, *Forgiveness and Reconciliation,*
p 1, Macmillan 1952

Today, Father, we lift to you all whose relationship with you has been broken by sin; all who have given up trying to return to you, perhaps because they are unable to forgive themselves; all who find it difficult to be reconciled with their family or friends and so find it hard also to be at one with you.

Stretch out your healing hand upon them, Christ our Healer and Saviour, and draw them to yourself; forgive them and restore them to fellowship with you, so they may know what it is to come to themselves and be reconciled with their brothers and sisters. Give them courage to take the first step and make the first move.

Then, Holy Spirit, shed the love of God abroad in their hearts, that men and women may take knowledge of them that they have been in your presence and so may feel better for being in theirs.

Grant us all to know this great joy of your forgiveness and the restoration to a richer relationship with you than we ever had before, unceasing because it is of you, O Holy Trinity, to whom be endless glory, praise and thanksgiving. Amen.

7 The door into the world

For if, when we were God's enemies, we were reconciled to him through the death of his Son, how much more, having been reconciled, shall we be saved through his life! Not only is this so, but we also rejoice in God through our Lord Jesus Christ, through whom we have now received reconciliation.

Romans 5: 10, 11

Heavenly Father, you have reconciled the world to yourself through the cross of your Son and have committed to your Church the ministry of reconciliation:
grant that we who bear witness to your reconciling word with our lips may also show your reconciling power in our lives, that the world may believe, to the glory of your name.   Amen.

New Every Morning, p 32, BBC

Christ crucified draw us to himself, to find in him a sure ground for faith, a firm support for hope, and the assurance of sins forgiven; and may the blessing of God almighty, the Father, the Son, and the Holy Spirit, be among us, and remain with us always.   Amen.

Blessing for Lent and Holy Week, ASB

DAY 12

FORTITUDE

1 *The entrance to the house of God's glory*

The Lord is the everlasting God,
the Creator of the ends of the earth.
He will not grow tired or weary,
and his understanding no one can fathom.
He gives strength to the weary,
and young men stumble and fall;
but those who hope in the Lord
will renew their strength.
They will soar on wings like eagles;
they will run and not grow weary,
they will walk and not faint.

Isaiah 40: 28–31

Eternal God and Father,
in whose presence we find rest and peace:
as we come to you now
may we be cleansed and strengthened by your
Spirit,
and serve you with a quiet mind,
to the glory of Jesus' name.   Amen.

New Every Morning, p 118, BBC

2 *The therapy room*

Father, I confess I have failed to trust you at every turn. I have allowed worries and anxieties to triumph over faith in you. And yet I know, in my best moments, that you have never let me down. Have mercy on me, forgive me and heal me from this faithlessness.

Give me strength in my inner being, born of the knowledge of your presence deep within me.

Give me *fortitude*, built on your gifts of dynamic faith and vibrant hope, so that today I may *boldly* approach the business of living, turning to you in every situation for your unfailing grace, knowing I shall go forth in your strength alone, made perfect in my weakness;

and may all love and all glory be yours, now and for ever.

Amen.

3 *The library*

The grace of Fortitude.

. . . the grace that makes men undertake hard things by their own will wisely and reasonably. There is something in the very name of Fortitude which speaks to the almost indelible love of heroism in men's hearts; but perhaps the truest Fortitude may often be a less heroic, a more tame and business-like affair than we are apt to think. It may be exercised chiefly in doing very little things, whose value lies in this, that, if one did not hope in God, one would not do them; in secretly dispelling moods which one would like to show; in saying nothing about one's lesser troubles and vexations; in seeing whether it may not be best to bear a burden before one tries to see whether one can shift it; in refusing one's self excuses which one would not refuse for others.

These are ways in which a man may every day be strengthening himself in the discipline of Fortitude; and then, if greater things are asked of him, he is not very likely to draw back from them. And while he waits the asking of these greater things, he may be gaining from the love of God a hidden strength and glory such as he himself would least of all suspect; he may be growing in the patience and perseverance of the saints. To go on choosing what has but a look of being the more excellent way, pushing on towards a faintly glimmering light, and never doubting the supreme worth of goodness even in its least brilliant fragments – this is the normal task of many lives; in this men show what they are like. And for this we need a quiet and sober Fortitude.

Francis Paget, Bishop of Oxford, *The Spirit of Discipline* pp 48f

4 *The music room*

O Jesus, I have promised
　　To serve thee to the end;
Be thou for ever near me,
　　My Master and my Friend:
I shall not fear the battle
　　If thou art by my side,
Nor wander from the pathway
　　If thou wilt be my guide.

O let me feel thee near me:
　　The world is ever near;
I see the sights that dazzle,
　　The tempting sounds I hear;
My foes are ever near me,
　　Around me and within;
But, Jesus, draw thou nearer,
　　And shield my soul from sin.

O let me hear thee speaking
　　In accents clear and still,
Above the storms of passion,
　　The murmurs of self-will;
O speak to reassure me,
　　To hasten or control;
O speak, and make me listen,
　　Thou guardian of my soul.

O Jesus, thou hast promised
　　To all who follow thee,
That where thou art in glory
　　There shall thy servant be;
And, Jesus, I have promised
　　To serve thee to the end:
O give me grace to follow,
　　My Master and my Friend.

O let me see thy foot-marks,
　　And in them plant mine own;
My hope to follow duly
　　Is in thy strength alone:
O guide me, call me, draw me,
　　Uphold me to the end;

And then in heaven receive me,
My Saviour and my Friend.
J. E. Bode, AMR 331

Of the many fine tunes, surely W. H. Ferguson's *Wolvercote*
excels. The masterly key change in the middle of the verse
adds greatly to the interpretation of the words. A veritable
prayer for Fortitude, at Confirmations or at any time of
life-change.

5 *The quiet room*

The Lord gives strength to his people;
the Lord blesses his people with peace.
Psalm 29: 11

* * * *

'. . . But the big courage is the cold-blooded kind, the
kind that never lets go even when you're feeling empty
inside, and your blood's thin, and there's no kind of fun
or profit to be had, and the trouble's not over in an hour
or two but lasts for months and years. One of the men
here was speaking about that kind, and he called it
"Fortitude". I reckon fortitude's the biggest thing a man
can have – just to go on enduring when there's no guts or
heart left in you. Billy had it when he trekked solitary
from Garungoze to the Limpopo with fever and a broken
arm just to show the Portugooses that he wouldn't be
downed by them. But the head man at the job was the
Apostle Paul . . .'

John Buchan, *Mr Standfast*
(Quoted by C. H. Dodd, *The Meaning of Paul for Today*,
Allen and Unwin 1920)

* * * *

St Paul gives an account of his fortitude and powers of
endurance in 2 Corinthians 11: 22–29. It is good to ponder
on this passage: comparing himself with other servants of
Christ (he admits it is foolish so to do) he claims: 'I have
worked much harder, been in prison more frequently, been
flogged more severely, and been exposed to death again

and again.' Perhaps even greater fortitude is needed for the spiritual problems: 'Besides everything else, I face daily the pressure of my concern for all the churches.' Here is an experience common to all Christian leaders.

But the experience on the other side of the coin is just as real. St Paul points to the grace of God granted to us in moments of weakness in a passage earlier in the same epistle. Read 2 Corinthians 6: 1–10, especially the last verse: 'sorrowful, yet always rejoicing; poor, yet making many rich; having nothing, and yet possessing everything.'

* * * *

The LORD is the stronghold of my life –
of whom shall I be afraid?

Psalm 27: 1b

6 *The living room*

O God, our Father, we know so well the infirmity and the weakness of this human life.

Strengthen the weakness of our faith, and give us trust for our trembling and hope for our fears.

Strengthen the weakness of our wills, that we may ever be strong enough to choose the right and to resist the wrong.

Strengthen the weakness of our decision, that we may no longer halt between two opinions.

Strengthen the weakness of our loyalty, that we may never again be ashamed to show whose we are and whom we serve.

Strengthen the weakness of our love, that we may come at last to love you as you have first loved us.

O God, our Father, we know so well the weakness of our bodies.

Keep us in good health; but, if illness and pain come to us, give us patience and cheerful endurance and healing in the end. And, as the years take from us strength of body, give us peace of heart and serenity of mind.

O God, our Father, we know so well the weakness and the insecurity of our hold upon this life.

In life we are in the midst of death. Comfort us when dear and loved ones are taken from us, and at such a time give us the glorious and immortal hope of life eternal as well as the sad memories of mortal loss. And deliver us from the fear of death, so that we may look on death as the gateway to eternal life for ever with our Lord.

Grant us all through life your all-sufficient grace that your power may ever be made perfect in our weakness; through Jesus Christ our Lord.   Amen.

William Barclay, *Prayers for the Christian Year*, SCM Press 1964

7 The door into the world

Father, hear the prayer we offer;
    Not for ease that prayer shall be,
But for strength that we may ever
    Live our lives courageously.

Not for ever in green pastures
    Do we ask our way to be;
But the steep and rugged pathway
    May we tread rejoicingly.

Not for ever by still waters
    Would we idly rest and stay;
But would smite the living fountains
    From the rocks along our way.

Be our Strength in hours of weakness,
    In our wanderings be our Guide;
Through endeavour, failure, danger,
    Father, be thou at our side.

Mrs L. M. Willis (1864), EH 385

Lord, may your strength always be made perfect in our weakness, and may it enfold us and all whom we meet this day.   Amen.

DAY 13

HEALING IN THE CHURCH

1 *The entrance to the house of God's glory*

> Now you are the body of Christ, and each one of you is a part of it. And in the church God has appointed . . . also those having gifts of healing, those able to help others. . .
>
> 1 Corinthians 12: 27f

If there is both truth and importance in the concept of Christian healing, then *what are we going to do about it?* It was a question I had to face for myself and still have to face. The effectiveness of today's Church and tomorrow's Church depends to a large extent on our answer to that question. Is the Church prepared, are we prepared to be available to the healing power of Christ? Will we admit our need, our sickness? Will we admit his power? Will we hear his call to channel his healing into this sick world at every level?
'Faithful is he who calls.' How faithful are we?

Lord Jesus, who chose twelve disciples and sent them forth to preach the gospel and to heal the sick:
Forgive the faithless disobedience of your children, and help us to restore the healing ministry to your Church.
Grant that your whole Church as your body may be inspired to teach and to heal; that again signs may follow upon faith in you, and the world may know that you are our mighty Saviour;
to whom be all praise and glory, now and for evermore. Amen.

Guild of Health, PP 999

2 *The therapy room*

The principle of forgiveness enshrined in the words of
the Lord's Prayer 'forgive us our trespasses as we forgive
those who trespass against us' operates in every sphere
of human relationships. How many relationships both in
the Church and outside it are ruined because of lack of
forgiveness. When I refuse to forgive someone who has
wronged me I allow a root of bitterness to grow in me
which may manifest itself in all kinds of mental and
physical hurt. Indeed I have known people who have
suffered severe physical disability through not having
forgiven or been forgiven. God knows and grieves over
the ways in which we hurt each other in so many ways.
Very often in my experience as a marriage counsellor I
have met a couple whose marriage has become so sour
that love has turned to hate. Almost always it has begun
with something fairly small and to the outsider apparently trivial. Because it has been allowed to go unhealed
and unforgiven it has grown into a festering sore that is
almost impossible to heal. Isn't this so often the case in
the Church too. A little division occurs which if not dealt
with in time becomes something really hurtful and makes
the Church's witness ineffectual and brings shame on the
name of Christ . . .

When the Church becomes a place of healing we won't
have to go out and persuade people to come in; our
problem will be finding time to deal with all who want to
come.

Cecil Kerr, *Power to Love* pp 146 ff, Christian Journals Ltd 1976

Our Father . . .

Lord, help us to become your healing people and the
Church to be a place of healing.   Amen.

3 *The library*

Let the Church have its psychological clinics. I strongly
recommend this. But Christ did not send out His
Apostles to be psychologists and doctors, but to be the

spearheads of fellowships made one through a discipline of prayer and corporate worship. At high temperatures even alien metals will fuse into an alloy, stronger than any constituent in it taken by itself. The love of God *can* do that for members of a fellowship who have temperamentally little in common and who, by themselves, must fail to heal, or even impress.

The way forward for the Church, then, seems clear. Let it support all that is being done to heal men through every known scientific means, but let it not be bluffed into supposing that that is the healing work it is called to do.

Many healing works carried on today, even in the name of religion, are only spasmodic and sporadic illustrations of ill-regulated and half-understood psychological phenomena. Many (so-called) 'healings' wrought often by cranks and charlatans illustrate the power of the mind over the body, rather than the kind of thing Christ did and calls His Church to do. We know that by examining what lies behind the cures.

True spiritual healing demands another kind of preparation altogether. Let a fellowship be formed of convinced, devout and sensible people. Let them regularly pray together. It may be necessary for them to live together for periods. We forget that the disciples lived together for three years, and *lived with Jesus*, and even then were weak and undependable. When all animosities, jealousies, ambitions, prejudices, suspicions and the like have been purged away within the fellowship; when the members of the fellowship have become one, both in flaming love to Christ and an unselfish desire to help others, then they can with confidence claim to be an extension of Christ's body, a part of '*the* Church, which is His Body,' and an instrument which the Holy Spirit can use in the ministry of direct spiritual healing.

Leslie Weatherhead, *Psychology, Religion and Healing*, p 490, Hodder 1951

4 *The music room*

A song of ascents. Of David

How good and pleasant it is
    when brothers live together in unity!
It is like precious oil poured on the head,
    running down on the beard,
  running down on Aaron's beard,
    down upon the collar of his robes.
It is as if the dew of Hermon
    were falling on Mount Zion.
For there the Lord bestows his blessing,
    even life for evermore.
Glory be . . .

Psalm 133

5 *The quiet room*

The rediscovery by the Church of her healing ministry,
seems to find its significance when seen as an integral
part of the unfolding of God's plan for His creation and
especially for His Church. For though we say we are
rediscovering our healing ministry, it is more true to say
that it is the Holy Spirit Who is restoring it. In other
words, this is a phenomenon *that is happening to us*. You
and I are caught up in it. And not only we, but also
our fellow-Christians throughout the world are being
touched by this same movement of the Spirit. This
'rediscovery' is universal. This phenomenon is happening to all the Churches throughout the world.

George Bennett, *Commissioned to Heal*, p 58,
Arthur James 1979

In our quiet time let us seek to experience 'this same
movement of the Spirit'.
The Holy Spirit IS restoring to the Church its healing
    ministry.
As members of the Body of Christ, this IS happening to us.
It IS happening to our fellow-Christians throughout the
    world.

*   *   *   *

All love, all glory, be to God that we are caught up
    in this movement of the Holy Spirit.
All love, all glory, be to God that it is happening
    not only to us but to all our fellow-Christians.
All love, all glory, be to God that HIS healing is
    'happening to all the Churches throughout the
    world.'

* * * *

Let us rest in the Holy Spirit who restores the
  healing power of God in the world
               – in the Church,
               – in me.

Thanks be to God for his indescribable gift.
  Amen.

2 Corinthians 9: 15

6 *The living room*

Luke describes the lifestyle of the first Christian healing
community as follows:

*They devoted themselves to the apostles' teaching and to the
fellowship, to the breaking of bread and to prayer.*

Acts 2: 42

Let us pray for our own church, local, national and international, that it may give priority to these four factors in its
lifestyle today:

Father, as your Son asked, we pray you will constantly send
your Holy Spirit to lead us into all truth.
May *those who teach* make that truth their own.
May those who listen hear your word through theirs.
May all be healed into a likeness to the mind of Christ.
  Amen.
Father, we thank you for the privilege of being part of the
Body of your Son, *the fellowship of the Holy Spirit*.
Give us a oneness in prayer out of which is born an
awareness of the boundlessness of your grace. So may we
truly become your community, able to contain and heal the
hurts and fears of all, a true fellowship of healing, prayer
and praise. Amen.

Father, your Son pronounced a blessing on those who hunger and thirst after righteousness, a right relationship with you. Give us such a hunger and thirst for the sacrament of his Body and Blood, that, as he makes himself known to us in *the breaking of bread*, we may receive such healing as will make us channels of his healing power for others, for they will know we have been with Jesus your Son. Amen.

Father, your Son taught his disciples to pray to you as Father; give us *a persistence and true devotion in prayer*, not only for our sake nor only for the sake of those for whom we pray, but for your sake, that the healing community of your Son may through the process of your Holy Spirit truly become a healed and healing community, empowered to carry forward the work of your Kingdom towards a healed creation. Amen.

7 The door into the world

> May the grace of Christ our Saviour,
> And the Father's boundless love,
> With the Holy Spirit's favour,
> Rest upon us from above.
>
> Thus may we abide in union
> With each other and the Lord,
> And possess, in sweet communion,
> Joys which earth cannot afford.
> John Newton (1725–1807), AMR 636

O Lord Jesus Christ, who said to your Apostles, My peace I leave with you, my peace I give unto you: regard not our sins, but the faith of your Church; and grant her that peace and unity which is according to your will, who lives and reigns with the Father and the Holy Spirit, one God, world without end. Amen.

SU

Christ the Good Shepherd, who laid down his life for the sheep, draw us and all who hear his voice to be one within one fold; and may the blessing of God almighty, the Father, the Son, and the Holy Spirit, be among us, and remain with us always. Amen.

Alternative blessing for Unity, ASB

DAY 14

HOPE

1 *The entrance to the house of God's glory*

You have been my hope, O Sovereign Lord,
   my confidence since my youth.
From birth I have relied on you;
   you brought me forth from my mother's womb.
I will ever praise you.
I have become like a portent to many,
   but you are my strong refuge.
My mouth is filled with your praise,
   declaring your splendour all the day long.

Psalm 71: 5–8

I am a man of hope, not for human reasons nor from any
natural optimism, but because I believe the Holy Spirit is
at work in the Church and in the World, even when His
name remains unheard.

Cardinal Leon Joseph Suenens

Lord God,
the scripture says you make all things new.
Make all things new this day.
Give us such hope in you
that we become optimistic about everyone and
   everything else,
Lord of all hopefulness, Lord of the future,
lead us forward with a light step and a courageous
   heart;
to your honour and glory,
and for the sake of Jesus Christ,
your Son, our Saviour.   Amen.

Jamie Wallace, HBCP 512

2 *The therapy room*

How much you have loved us, O good Father, who spared not even your own Son, but delivered him up for us wicked men. How you have loved us, for whom he who thought it not robbery to be equal with you became obedient even unto the death on the cross, he who alone was free among the dead, having power to lay down his life and power to take it up again: for us he was to you both victor and victim, and victor because victim: for us he was to you both priest and sacrifice, and priest because sacrifice: turning us from slaves into your sons, by being your Son and becoming a slave. *Rightly is my hope strong in him*, who sits at your right hand and intercedes for us; otherwise I should despair. For many and great are my infirmities, many and great; but *your medicine is of more power*. We might well have thought your Word remote from union with man and so have despaired of ourselves, if he had not been made flesh and dwelt among us . . .

See, Lord, I cast my care upon you, that I may live: and I will consider the wondrous things of your law. You know my unskilfulness and my infirmity: *teach me and heal me*. He your only One, in whom are hidden all the treasures of wisdom and knowledge, has redeemed me with his blood.

St Augustine, *The Confessions*

3 *The library*

When on a pilgrimage, we are encouraged to keep going because we have the end of the journey to look forward to. We have already now enjoyed in prospect something of the joy we shall have in reality at the end of the journey. We can look forward to good things, to good times. That is the reason why Christians should always be joyful, always cheerful. They have hope. Hope is the confidence that we shall find what we are looking for, and will reach the point we are aiming at. That confidence comes from God. It is He who makes our dreams come true, who satisfies our deepest aspirations, who gives us total fulfilment.

Hope is a Christian virtue and it is as important as faith and charity. This is not said often enough. People probably hear many sermons on faith and love, but not many on hope. Rarely do we see an article on hope, or see commended to us the importance of being cheerful and happy, in spite of the trials of life, in spite of the difficulties we meet. A true Christian would perhaps say 'because of the trials, because of the difficulties'. There has to be in every Christian life a certain joy, a certain peace. I believe many people are depressed more than they should be by the conventions of our mass media. Good news does not sell newspapers, does not make dramatic television pictures. But the unrelieved diet of dramatic crises, of tragedies and conflict, leave many, especially the housebound, the elderly and the nervous, with ample grounds for pessimism and depression.

We must never fail to trust in the love of God, to have confidence that He wants our good. We must be convinced that He wants us, and wants us badly, if I may put it that way.

Basil Hume, OSB, Cardinal Archbishop of Westminster, *To Be a Pilgrim*, St Paul Publications

It is for this reason that Christians must continually be on the move to create signs of this new creation, signs of hope in a world without hope, signs of community in a disrupted world, signs of healing where there is disease, distress and disunity. The early Christians were quick to realise the needs of their time. In a world that had gone away from God, they knew they had to live a sign of God's presence. The Holy Spirit of movement, unity and truth, led them, as we read in those early chapters of Acts, to be such a sign in a disbelieving world, such a light in the darkness of violent disbelief. We read how 'they devoted themselves to the apostles' teaching and to the fellowship, to the breaking of bread and to prayer' (Acts 2: 42). I have always felt this to be one of the most important words given to us from Scripture. Here was the framework for the lifestyle of the Christian community, whose destiny was to be a sign of the unity of all creation. Every part of it spoke of a relationship with God through Christ in the power of the Spirit, lived out in the

service of humanity until God was all in all. The teaching,
fellowship, breaking of bread, prayer – all pointed
Godward and drew the believer into a relationship with
Christ in God in order to fulfil his essential destiny as a
living part of creation, to be fully human and fully alive.

M. M., *Journey to the Wholeness*, pp 87f, SPCK 1986

4 *The music room*

All my hope on God is founded;
   he doth still my trust renew.
Me through change and chance he guideth,
   only good and only true.
      God unknown,
      He alone
Calls my heart to be his own.

Pride of man and earthly glory,
   sword and crown betray his trust;
What with care and toil he buildeth,
   tower and temple, fall to dust.
      But God's power,
      Hour by hour,
Is my temple and my tower.

God's great goodness aye endureth,
   deep his wisdom, passing thought:
Splendour, light, and life attend him,
   beauty springeth out of naught.
      Evermore
      From his store
New-born worlds rise and adore.

Still from man to God eternal
   sacrifice of praise be done,
High above all praises praising
   for the gift of Christ his Son.
      Christ doth call
      One and all:
Ye who follow shall not fall.

Robert Bridges (1844–1930),
based on the German of J. Neander (1650–80), HFT 3

5 *The quiet room*

The woman with a haemorrhage: Mark 5: 25–34

Here was a woman who placed all her hope in the healing power of Jesus Christ. He was actually on his way to Jairus's daughter when his attention was diverted by a consciousness that power had been drained from him. The woman, with a long medical history, had come up behind him in the crowd and touched his clothes. Deeply in her being she knew that *If I just touch his clothes, I will be healed.* The Hebrew conception of personality extended beyond a person to his shadow, footprints or clothes.

To the disciples' slight irritation, he insisted on finding this woman in the crowd. He could have left the matter there, a woman healed of her physical disability. But the hope he holds out to humankind is complete healing, a new wholeness of personality. For her salvation/healing she needed to meet Jesus.

* * * *

At last she came forward and *told him the whole truth.* She unloaded all her resentments and fears, her guilt feelings and inadequacies on Jesus. She became healed inwardly, a whole person. She was not disappointed of her hope: *Daughter, your faith has healed you. Go in peace and be freed from your suffering.*

* * * *

The healing we seek is the physical and yet more than the physical. It is a personal encounter with Christ the Healer, leading to a new wholeness of being. This is the hope he holds out to us all.

* * * *

A text for today: *Set your hope fully on the grace to be given you when Jesus Christ is revealed.*
1 Peter 1: 13

6 *The living room*

O God, the creator and preserver of all mankind,
we pray for men of every race,
and in every kind of need:
make your ways known on earth,
your saving power among all nations.
   Especially we pray for . . .
We pray for your Church throughout the world:
guide and govern us by your Holy Spirit,
that all who profess and call themselves Christians
may be led into the way of truth,
and hold the faith in unity of spirit
in the bond of peace, and in righteousness of life.
   Especially we pray for . . .
We commend to your fatherly goodness
all who are anxious or distressed in mind or body;
comfort or relieve them in their need;
give them patience in their sufferings,
and bring good out of their troubles.
   Especially we pray for . . .
Merciful Father,
accept these prayers
for the sake of your Son,
our Saviour Jesus Christ.   Amen.

               Alternative form of intercession.
          The Order for Holy Communion Rite A, ASB

7 *The door into the world*

Why are you downcast, O my soul?
Why so disturbed within me?
Put your hope in God,
for I will yet praise him,
my Saviour and my God.

               Psalm 42: 11

Lord, Give us this day,
   Forgiveness for the past;
   Courage for the present;
   Hope for the future,

And in your infinite mercy come to meet our
   infinite need; through Jesus Christ our
   Lord.   Amen.
      William Barclay, *Prayers for the Christian Year*,
                                    SCM Press 1964

May the God of hope fill you with all joy and peace as
you trust in him, so that you may overflow with hope by
the power of the Holy Spirit.   Amen.
                                    Romans 15: 13

DAY 15

HUMILITY

1 *The entrance to the house of God's glory*

If you have any encouragement from being united with Christ, if any comfort from his love, if any fellowship with the Spirit, if any tenderness and compassion, then make my joy complete by being like-minded, having the same love, being one in spirit and purpose. Do nothing out of selfish ambition or vain conceit, but *in humility* consider others better than yourselves.

Philippians 2: 1f

At times it is important to remember just how small we are. Franklin D. Roosevelt used to have a little ritual with the famous naturalist, William Beebe. After an evening's chat, the two men would go outside and look into the night sky. Gazing into the stars, they would find the lower left-hand corner of the great square of Pegasus. One of them would recite these words, as part of their ritual: 'That is a spiral galaxy of Andromeda. It is as large as our Milky Way. It is one of a hundred million galaxies. It is 750,000 light-years away. It consists of 100 billion suns, each larger than our sun.' They would then pause, and Roosevelt would finally say, 'Now I think we feel small enough. Let us go to bed!'

David Watson, In Search of God,
Kingsway Publications Ltd, 1974

O Lord, our Lord
   how majestic is your name in all the earth!
When I consider your heavens
   the work of your fingers,
the moon and the stars,

which you have set in place,
what is man that you are mindful of him,
  the son of man that you care for him?
O Lord, our Lord,
  how majestic is your name in all the earth!

Psalm 8: 1, 3, 4, 9

2 *The therapy room*

A great physician has come to us and forgiven all of our sins. If we prefer to be ill again, we shall not only harm ourselves but be ungrateful to that physician.

Let us follow his ways, then, as he has shown them to us, *particularly that of humility*, since he became himself that way for us. He showed us the way of humility by his counsels and followed it by suffering for us. The Word was incapable of dying, but in order to be able to die for us he became flesh and dwelt among us. The immortal one took on mortality to die for us and by his death to destroy ours.

The Lord did this; he gave us this boon. Though he was great, he was humbled. Being humbled, he was put to death. Put to death, he rose again and was exalted. And so he will not leave us among the dead. As in this life he has raised us up in our faith and confession as just men, so he will raise us up in himself in the resurrection of the dead. *He gave us humility as a way*. If we follow it, we shall give thanks to the Lord and sing with good reason: 'We give thanks to you, O God; we give thanks and call on your name.'

St Augustine, Sermon 23A

Lord Jesus, keep us in the way of your self-forgetting humility and make us whole.   Amen.

3 *The library*

Humility is central to the Christian life; it is fundamental. It is a virtue that fits one to be a religious person. It is a virtue not only for monastic life, but for all Christian life.

Humility is not modesty, though modesty is one of its signs. It includes having a low opinion of oneself; it is facing the truth about who God is, and the truth of who I am.

Humility in another is a very beautiful thing to see; but the attempt to become humble is painful indeed. It hurts. It hurts to be criticised, to be misunderstood, to be misjudged, to be snubbed, to be written off; but such things are the high road to humility. None of us enjoys walking that way. Oddly enough, I believe that for some of us it is when we realise how little we are regarded by others that we begin to recognise how highly we are esteemed by God. We have ceased to wonder what others think about us; we have discovered our worth in the eyes of our Father.

*   *   *   *

At some time in our lives, we may feel that we are failures. We have experienced great disappointments, and the sense of being less good than we should be, of being less successful than we would like to be. This sense of failure and inadequacy is common among us. Our Lord must have felt like this at the end of his life. Everybody had turned against him. They were going to execute him; they were insulting him. We know that this moment of failure was God's moment of success. That is a most important fact to learn. Whenever I feel inadequate or a failure, disappointed or upset, God can enter into my life, and bring His success.

*   *   *   *

Basil Hume, OSB, Cardinal Archbishop of Westminster,
To Be a Pilgrim, St Paul Publications

4 *The music room*

The following was in all probability part of an early Christian hymn, quoted by St Paul in this letter:

Your attitude should be the same as that of Christ Jesus:
Who, being in very nature God,

did not consider equality with God
>> something to be grasped,
but made himself nothing,
>> taking the very nature of a servant,
>> being made in human likeness.
And being found in appearance as a man,
>> he humbled himself
>> and became obedient to death –
>> even death on a cross!
Therefore God exalted him to the highest place
>> and gave him the name that is above every
>> name,
that at the name of Jesus every knee should bow,
>> in heaven and on earth and under the earth,
and every tongue confess that Jesus Christ is Lord,
>> to the glory of God the Father.

>> Philippians 2: 5–11

5 *The quiet room*

In our quiet moments today, let us focus on the way Jesus
chose for himself – the path of humility:

>> He made himself nothing
>> >> taking the very nature of a servant . . .
>> He humbled himself
>> >> and became obedient to death –
>> >> even death on a cross!

>> Philippians 2: 7f

* * * *

St Francis of Assisi was among those who have followed the
Master most closely in this regard:

>> For this reason
>> Francis,
>> the model of humility,
>> wanted his friars to be called Minor
>> and the superiors of his Order to be called servants,
>> in order to use the very words of the Gospel
>> which he had promised to observe
>> and in order that his followers
>> might learn from this very name

that they had come to the school
of the humble Christ
to learn humility.
Jesus Christ
the teacher of humility,
instructed his disciples in true humility
by saying: *'Whoever wishes to become great among you,*
let him be your servant;
and whoever wishes to be first among you
will be your slave.'
St Bonaventure, *The Life of St Francis*, approved as the official
biography at the General Chapter of Paris in 1266

* * * *

Reflect – that true humility consists to a great extent in
being ready for what the Lord desires to do with you, and
happy that He should do it; and in always considering
yourselves unworthy to be called His servants.

St Teresa of Avila

6 *The living room*

It is good for me to be humiliated.

Pope John XXIII

Lord, I bring before you today all in positions of
power:
– in national and local government;
– in industry and commerce;
– in trade unions and the media;
– in the churches and the caring professions.
Grant to each of them the healing balm of humility:
– a wisdom that knows it is your authority they
wield;
– a compassion that enables them to care for all;
– a holy fear that leads them to approach their
task with reverence and awe;
– a humble gratitude for the task they have been
given;
– a lowliness that asks for nothing but to give
and serve.

May all experience your healing in themselves
and, keeping their relationships healthy and
   whole,
acknowledge you reign as Lord over all;
   for yours is the Kingdom, the power and the
   glory,
      for ever and ever.   Amen.

O Lord, we pray for humility for ourselves. Help us to
lose our self-importance, and to see that we often fuss
about things that don't really matter. We thank you for
the gift of humour; may we laugh at ourselves sometimes, and get things into proportion. Preserve us from
false humility and pride. Help us to appreciate what we
have, and not to be always wanting something else. Let
us pray for the 'have-nots', the poor and the lonely, and
think what we might do to help.   Amen.

Sue Jeffreys

7 The door into the world

Clothe yourselves with humility towards one another,
because
   'God opposes the proud
   but gives grace to the
      humble.'
Humble yourselves, therefore, under God's mighty
hand, that he may lift you up in due time.

1 Peter 5: 5, 6

And give me, good Lord, an humble, lowly, quiet, peace-
able, patient, charitable, kind and filial and tender mind,
every shade, in fact, of charity, with all my words and all
my works and all my thoughts, to have a taste of thy holy
blessed Spirit.   Amen.

St Thomas More (1478–1535)

And the God of all grace, who called you to his eternal glory in Christ, after you have suffered a little while,
will himself restore you and make you strong, firm
and steadfast. To him be the power for ever and ever.
Amen.

1 Peter 5: 10, 11

DAY 16

INNER HEALING

1 *The entrance to the house of God's glory*

> Praise the Lord, O my soul;
>> all my inmost being, praise his holy name.
> Praise the Lord, O my soul,
>> and forget not all his benefits –
> who forgives all your sins
>> and heals all your diseases,
> who redeems your life from the pit
>> and crowns you with love and compassion,
> who satisfies your desires with good things
>> so that your youth is renewed like the eagle's.
>
> Psalm 103: 1–5

Lord, open our hearts to receive your gift of grace, the love that releases us from our bondage and gives us freedom:

> freedom from cares and worries that stifle our happiness;
>
> freedom from sins that cling to us, and to which we cling;
>
> freedom from all that prevents our becoming what we can be and ought to be.

So bring us, O Lord, to the experience of life more abundant, for your name's sake. Amen.

New Every Morning, p 47, BBC

2 *The therapy room*

Praying for inner healing

1 The first step is to ask, with as much faith as you have, that the Lord heal you interiorly:

> Lord, you have told us to ask and we will receive, to seek and we will find, to knock and you will open the door to us. I ask you now for inner healing. Heal me, make me whole. I trust in your personal love for me and in the healing power of your compassion.

2 The second step is repentance, a turning to the Lord for forgiveness. Coming into the light of his love and understanding, I am free to see myself as I really am and to become more aware of the sin, the disorder, and the hurts and the wounds inside me. I am free, in the Lord's love, to see better my need for forgiveness and for inner healing.

> Lord, I am sorry for all my sins, and I trust in your mercy. With your help, I renounce my sins and any sinful patterns in my life; I renounce everything that in any way opposes you. I accept with all my heart your forgiving love. And I ask you for the grace to be aware of the disorder in my inner self, to experience my own interior disorder with my wounds and hurts and sinfulness.
>
> Guide me in this prayer; show me what to pray for and how to pray. Bring to my mind whatever pain or hurts you want me to ask you to heal.

3 Now, see what problem or painful experience comes to mind, and pray for healing regarding that problem or that memory. (If more than one thing comes to mind, take them one at a time.) It might be a failure or a broken friendship or the loss of a person you love. It could be something in childhood, such as a less than perfect relationship with your father or your mother. It could be present anger or depression or some undesirable behaviour pattern.

Pray in your own words, lifting up the hurt or the painful memory or the problem to the Lord for healing. Pray simply, like a child.

4 Forgive everyone involved, praying for them by name and telling the Lord that, with his help, you forgive each one. Imagine the person to be forgiven and, in your imagination, put your arms around the person and say, 'I forgive you.' Then see the Lord in your imagination, his arms outstretched to embrace you both, and – with one arm around the person you have forgiven – walk with that person into the Lord's arms and let him forgive you both and reconcile you to each other and to himself.

5 Picture in your imagination the situation the problem goes back to, or the place of the hurtful memory. Picture the Lord in that place and situation, filling it with his healing love, being with you there. And ask him to heal you, again praying simply and in your own words . . .

Robert Faricy, Praying for Inner Healing, pp 13f,
SCM Press 1979

Give me a candle of the Spirit, O God, as I go down into the deep of my own being. Show me the hidden things. Take me down to the spring of my life, and tell me my nature and name. Give me freedom to grow so that I may become the self, the seed of which thou didst plant in me at my making. Out of the deep I cry unto thee, O Lord. Amen.

George Appleton, One Man's Prayers, SPCK

* * * *

Have mercy on me, O God, according to your
    unfailing love;
according to your great compassion blot out my
    transgressions.
Wash away all my iniquity and cleanse me from
    my sin.
Surely you desire truth in the inner parts;
you teach me wisdom in the inmost place.
Cleanse me with hyssop, and I shall be clean;
wash me, and I shall be whiter than snow.
Let me hear joy and gladness;
let the bones you have crushed rejoice.
Hide your face from my sins and blot out all my
    iniquity.

Create in me a pure heart, O God,
and renew a steadfast spirit within me.
Do not cast me from your presence
or take your Holy Spirit from me.
Restore to me the joy of your salvation
and grant me a willing spirit, to sustain me.

Psalm 51: 1, 2, 6–12

3 The library

A testimony

In the spring of 1975 after ten years of suffering from a depressive illness which drugs and therapy would not alleviate, someone gave me a copy of, 'Miracle at Crowhurst', by George Bennett. At that time I did not know about this home of healing in the south of England, and the services that are regularly held there. I was very sceptical when I booked in to stay for a few days to receive the ministry of healing. I did not believe it would help me, after all, my illness had gone on for so long. I had lost all hope of recovery.

My first impression was the care that someone had taken to arrange flowers that greeted me in my bedroom. The beauty and love that they conveyed was a strength in itself.

During my stay I was led through a series of interviews with a priest in a very unpressurized way. This led me to make my confession, and receive anointing with Holy Oil. The priest was then accompanied by a female member of staff, and the three of us interceded for my healing, which included the healing of memories. I felt very loved, and supported by these people engaged in the ministry of healing, and was overwhelmed by the depth of God's love for me.

The recovery was gradual, but there had to be a definite readjustment over the next twelve months. I was now free from the depressive illness, and needed to arrange my life accordingly, which meant obtaining work. Healing brings with it a complete change of direction in some lives, when there is no longer the handicap of ill health or physical disability. Over the years I can praise God, that there has not been a recurrence of my depressive illness. I was healed on that lovely God-given day in the Chapel of Christ's Glory at Crowhurst.

Celia Russell, now a nurse

4 *The music room*

'I believe that through whatever changes and trans-formations music is passing it must unswervingly keep its idealistic aim; otherwise, it may cease to retain its mysterious power of healing and of giving joy, and just dwindle into an excitant aural sensation, and nothing more.'

'I demand from music not what I demanded as a young man, which was sound and sound only . . . I now demand enhancement of life.'

Sir Arthur Bliss, Master of the Queen's Musick (1953–75)
(Quoted by Michael Trend in *The Music Makers*,
Weidenfeld and Nicolson 1985)

Let us thank God for the pieces of music that have brought enhancement to our life . . .
Let us pray for all composers, conductors and performers that they may strive for such ideals and find such inspira-tion as will bring healing and joy to all who hear their sound.
Eternal Lord God, source of all beauty and harmony, we praise you for the gift of music:
    for the inspiration given to those who compose it,
    for the skill and devotion of those who perform it,
    and the faculties and powers which enable us to enjoy
      it;
and we pray that as by this gift our lives are enriched and renewed, so we may glorify you in a fuller dedication of ourselves, giving thanks always for all things
    in the name of our Lord Jesus Christ.   Amen.

New Every Morning, p 140, BBC 1973

5 *The quiet room*

The Samaritan woman at the well

You can read the story in John 4: 4–42, or just recall the
whole incident to mind. Watch how Jesus goes ever deeper
and deeper into the heart.

*   *   *   *

The Samaritan woman, encountering Jesus at the well,
experiences an interior healing. Jesus asks the woman for
water. In answer, she teases him for stepping outside the
bounds of social convention by speaking to her. Jesus
then invites her with a double invitation: 1) to recognize
him, and 2) to ask him for the living water. When she asks
him for the living water, Jesus brings to light the disorder
in her life, past and present, and a re-ordering of the
woman's life starts. She begins to recognize Jesus as the
Messiah, and he responds by affirming her recognition.
Converted, she uses her new freedom to announce the
good news to other Samaritans.

The meeting between Jesus and the Samaritan woman
describes the inner healing that takes place when we
meet the Lord. He invites us to recognize him as Saviour
and to ask him for the living water, for his Spirit who
guides and teaches us. The Lord reveals us to ourselves,
bringing to the light of his healing love the past and
present disorder in our lives. He converts us and heals
us, and sends us to others in the new freedom that comes
from accepting the living water.

Robert Faricy, *Praying*, SCM Press 1983

*   *   *   *

'The Woman of Samaria'

He came to me with his eyes and asked for water,
Stretched out his hands and spoke.
His mind burned into mine like the noon sun,
My pitcher of thoughts broke.

I had not noticed him at rest by the well-head,
Shadowed by the rare tree;
But as I carried my shame into its coolness
His eyes awaited me.

I tried to avoid them as I drew the well-rope
Taut through a mindless hand.
I saw his robe cross the speckled sunlight,
His feet stir the hot sand.

I saw his face. It was white with road-dust,
Whiter than any stone.
But his eyes were ageless and deep as well-shafts
As they met my own.

They unroofed my brain with their profound
　　gazing,
Made the heart a molten thing;
Every purdahed thought unveiled itself
Under their questioning.

He spoke of water to cleanse the spirit:
I tried not to understand.
He followed me along the road of my evasions,
And when it ceased in sand

He brought me home from my self-forced
　　journey –
He showed me my own soul
Cracked and dry as a discarded wine-skin,
And made it whole . . .

He came to me with his eyes and asked for water,
Stretched out his hands and spoke.
As I carried my peace back to the streets of Sychar,
A new world awoke.

                    Clive Sansom, *The Witnesses*, Methuen 1971

6 *The living room*

The unique capacity of the mind of Christ is to allow
maturity to evolve by providing the foundation of a
healed past . . . Our subconscious memory, a mental
computer, records everything. It forgets nothing. The
only means we have of revising this emotional record is
by the re-creative work of the Holy Spirit. And often the
Spirit must redo our earliest recollections.

Ruth Carter Stapleton, *The Experience of Inner Healing*, EB

O Lord God, I thank thee for the growing knowledge of myself, of the depths of personality which affect my thinking, my feeling, my behaviour, and my dreams. There is so much more than I ever thought, so much more to offer thee for the cleansing and sanctifying of the Spirit. Heal my inner divisions in the unity of thy will, set my fears at rest in the assurance of thy love and grace, let no resentments destroy my inner peace, no thoughts of self deflect me from thy purpose for me. Help me to grow towards the fullness of life and love seen in thy blessed Son, Jesus Christ my Lord. Amen.

George Appleton, *One Man's Prayers*, 42, SPCK 1967

Come, my Light, and illumine my darkness,
Come, my Life, and revive me from death.
Come my Physician, and heal my wounds.
Come, Flame of divine love, and burn up the
 thorns of my sins, kindling my heart with the
 flame of thy love.
Come, my King, sit upon the throne of my heart
 and reign there.
For thou alone art my King and my Lord.

St Dimitri of Rostov (17th century), OBP 5, Oxford 1985

7 The door into the world

Heal me, O Lord, and I shall be healed;
 save me and I shall be saved,
 for you are the one I praise.
Jeremiah 17: 14

If we want wholeness and holiness, Jeremiah's prayer will be found frequently on our lips. If there is health in the core of our personality, it will affect our whole being. And praise lies at the heart of inner health.

* * * *

Praise be to the God and Father of our Lord Jesus Christ, who has blessed us in the heavenly realms with every spiritual blessing in Christ. For he chose us in him before the creation of the world to be holy and blameless in his sight . . . For this reason I kneel before the Father, from whom the whole family in heaven and on earth derives its name. I pray that out of his glorious riches he may *strengthen you with power through his Spirit in your inner being*, so that Christ may dwell in your hearts through faith. And I pray that you, being rooted and established in love, may have power, together with all the saints, to grasp how wide and long and high and deep is the love of Christ, and to know this love that surpasses knowledge – that you may be filled to the measure of all the fulness of God.

Now to him who is able to do immeasurably more than all we ask or imagine, according to his power that is at work within us, to him be glory in the Church and in Christ Jesus throughout all generations, for ever and ever!   Amen.

Ephesians 1: 3, 4; 3: 14–21

DAY 17

JESUS OUR HEALTH

1 *The entrance to the house of God's glory*

Jesus went throughout Galilee, teaching in their syna-
gogues, preaching the good news of the kingdom, and
healing every disease and sickness among the people.
News about him spread all over Syria, and people
brought to him all who were ill with various diseases,
those suffering severe pain, the demon-possessed, the
epileptics and the paralytics, and he healed them.

Matthew 4: 23f

How sweet the name of Jesus sounds
  In a believer's ear!
It soothes his sorrows, heals his wounds,
  And drives away his fear.

It makes the wounded spirit whole,
  And calms the troubled breast;
'Tis manna to the hungry soul,
  And to the weary rest.

Dear name! the rock on which I build,
  My shield and hiding-place,
My never-failing treasury filled
  With boundless stores of grace.
        J. Newton (1725–1807), EH 405

May the holy name of Jesus be my health today and
always. Amen.

2 *The therapy room*

Almighty and most merciful Father; We have erred, and strayed from thy ways like lost sheep. We have followed too much the devices and desires of our own hearts. We have offended against thy holy laws. We have left undone those things which we ought to have done; And we have done those things which we ought not to have done; And there is no health in us. But thou, O Lord, have mercy upon us, miserable offenders. Spare thou them, O God, which confess their faults. Restore thou them that are penitent; According to thy promises declared unto mankind in Christ Jesus our Lord. And grant, O most merciful Father, for his sake; That we may hereafter live a godly, righteous, and sober life, To the glory of thy holy Name.   Amen.

General confession at Morning and Evening Prayer, BCP

3 *The library*

In addition to emotion, intellect and will, human personality has a spiritual nature. This has sometimes been called a 'God hunger', i.e. a sense of the infinite – 'Our hearts are restless till they rest in Thee', a restlessness very evident in the present day. For this reason Christian healing has a vital part to play in cooperation with other skills for the wholeness of man. In the entirety of both his present and his potential personality man is known only to his creator. Christ came to make men whole.

All consideration of the Christian healing ministry today must be seen within this wider context, for it is not the removal of symptoms that is in question, but the healing of the whole person . . .

The Christian speaks of a new nature, of yet another factor introduced into the life of man, not by evolution but by the incarnation of Christ, raising him by regeneration to membership of the Body of Christ, which is a divinization of man, leading him to a yet greater goal. In this new nature are laws not so readily applicable to the old; what to the latter seem miracles may have a 'natural' place here.

If this regenerate life throws light on the way ahead, if this is the way of progress, life according to its laws will give harmony and thus health and wholeness to man, as well as meaning and direction to the present. Such laws are shown by the life, death and resurrection of Christ to be not legalistic codes but basically the law of love calling for self-sacrifice, of life through death.

Since it is to the attainment of man's potential that he must ever strive and not just drift with the tide, it is vital to his well-being to press forward; and it is Christ who claims to be the way, the truth and the life by which mankind in him may attain the goal, until, as St Paul expresses it: 'We become the perfect Man, fully mature with the fullness of Christ himself'. (Ephesians 4: 13).

Dame Raphael Frost, *Christ and Wholeness*, pp 8, 10,
James Clarke 1985

4 *The music room*

O for a thousand tongues to sing
  My dear Redeemer's praise,
The glories of my God and King,
  The triumphs of his grace!

Jesus – the name that charms our fears,
  That bids our sorrows cease;
'Tis music in the sinner's ears,
  'Tis life, *and health*, and peace.

He breaks the power of cancelled sin,
  He sets the prisoner free;
His Blood can make the foulest clean;
  His Blood availed for me.

He speaks; – and, listening to his voice,
  New life the dead receive,
The mournful broken hearts rejoice,
  The humble poor believe.

Hear him, ye deaf; his praise, ye dumb,
  Your loosened tongues employ;
Ye blind, behold your Saviour come;
  And leap, ye lame, for joy!

My gracious Master and my God,
　　Assist me to proclaim
And spread through all the earth abroad
　　The honours of thy name.
Charles Wesley (1707–1788), EH 446

5 *The quiet room*

'Now I write a song of love that you shall delight in when
you are loving Jesus Christ:

Jesus, Jesus, Jesus,
For thee it is I long;
Therefore, my life and my living,
Thou art my only song.

Jesus, my dear and beloved,
Delight art thou to sing;
Jesus, my mirth and melody,
When wilt thou come, my King?

Jesus, my health and my honey,
My joy without ceasing;
Jesus, I covet for to die,
When it is thy pleasing.

Jesus, my hope and my health,
My joy for evermore:
Be thou my burning zeal,
That I thy love may feel,
And dwell with thee in wealth.

Jesus, with thee I am strong:
Better it were to die
Than all this world to own
And have it in mastery.

Jesus, my saviour,
Jesus, my comforter,
Of all fairness the flower,
My help and my succour:
When may I see thy bower?

My song is in sighing,
My life is longing,

Until I see my King,
So fair in his shining,
So fair in his beauty.'
Richard Rolle (*c.* 1300–1349), a Yorkshire hermit.
(Translated by John G. Harrell, SPCK 1963)

Ponder for a few moments on the phrases in italics as you absorb them into your consciousness.

6 *The living room*

When the sun was setting, the people brought to Jesus all who had various kinds of sickness, and laying his hands on each one, he healed them.

Luke 4: 40

Almighty God, in the name of Jesus your Son,
who healed the sick and consoled the sad,
we pray for all who suffer –
– through sickness of body or mind . . .
– through fear or depression . . .
– through loneliness or bereavement . . .
and we ask that according to your will
they may be healed and comforted,
for the sake of Jesus Christ our Lord.   Amen.
New Every Morning, p 32, BBC

Lord, I specially bring before you today . . .

Lord, he/she whom you love is sick

* * * *

Lord of all compassion,
whose hand is ever stretched out
in blessing and healing upon the sick;
Look upon these your servants
we have named before you,
that they may be set free
from the sickness which afflicts them,
and be healed by your power,
for the glory of your name,
Jesus Christ, our Saviour and Healer.   Amen.
Guild of Health (adapted)

7 *The door into the world*

Trust in the Lord with all your heart
   and lean not on your own understanding;
in all your ways acknowledge him,
   and he will make your paths straight.
Do not be wise in your own eyes;
   fear the Lord and shun evil.
This will bring health to your body
   and nourishment to your bones.

Proverbs 3: 5–8

Make us always thankful, our heavenly Father,
   for your most precious gift of health;
for our sight, our speech, our hearing;
   for all the powers of body and mind
   which enable us to enjoy life to the full.
Teach us to safeguard the health that is ours;
   and deepen our compassion for those who suffer
      illness;
and help us to use the days of our strength
   in your service and for your glory;
   through Jesus Christ our Lord.   Amen.

Frank Colquhoun, CPP 455

Give us a sense of humour, Lord,
   and also things to laugh about.
Give us the grace to take a joke against ourselves
   and to see the funny side of life.
Save us from annoyance, bad temper,
   or resentfulness against our friends.
Help us to laugh even in the face of trouble;
   and fill our minds with the love of Jesus,
      for his name's sake.   Amen.

A. G. Bullivant, NPP 574

Father, preserve me in your love,
Jesus, be my health,
Spirit, give me strength and wisdom,
   now, and all my days.   Amen.

DAY 18
JOY

1 *The entrance to the house of God's glory*

Praise be to the God and Father of our Lord Jesus Christ! In his great mercy he has given us new birth into a living hope through the resurrection of Jesus Christ from the dead, and into an inheritance that can never perish, spoil or fade – kept in heaven for you, who through faith are shielded by God's power until the coming of the salvation that is ready to be revealed in the last time. *In this you greatly rejoice*, though now for a little while you may have had to suffer grief in all kinds of trials. These have come so that your faith – of greater worth than gold, which perishes even though refined by fire – may be proved genuine and may result in praise, glory and honour when Jesus Christ is revealed. Though you have not seen him, you love him; and even though you do not see him now, you believe in him and are *filled with an inexpressible and glorious joy*, for you are receiving the goal of your faith, the salvation (healing) of your souls.

1 Peter 1: 3–9

We are all strings in the concert of his joy.

Jakob Boehme, HBCQ

You have made known to me the path of life;
you will *fill me with joy* in your presence,
with eternal pleasures at your right hand.

Psalm 16: 11

Almighty God, in whose presence is the fullness of joy,

and whose power is made perfect in our weakness:
enable us so to dwell in your presence
that we may have your peace in our hearts;
and so to rest on your strength
that we may have victory over evil;
through Jesus Christ our Lord.   Amen.

New Every Morning, p 94, BBC

2 *The therapy room*

O God, Thou art Life, Wisdom, Truth, Bounty, and
Blessedness, the Eternal, the only true Good. My God
and my Lord, Thou art my hope and *my heart's joy*.

I confess, with thanksgiving, that Thou hast made me
in Thine image, that I may direct all my thoughts to Thee,
and love Thee.

Lord, make me to know Thee aright, that I may more
and more love, enjoy, and possess Thee. And since, in
the life here below, I cannot fully attain this blessedness,
let it at least grow in me day by day, until it all be fulfilled
at last in the life to come.

Here be the knowledge of Thee increased, and there let
it be perfected. Here let my love of Thee grow, and there
let it ripen; that my joy being here great in hope, may
there in fruition be made perfect.   Amen.

St Anselm (1033–1109)

Christ was anointed with the spiritual oil of gladness,
that is with the Holy Spirit, who is called the oil of
gladness, because he is the author of spiritual joy; and
you have been anointed with chrism because you have
become sharers of Christ.

Instructions to the newly baptized at Jerusalem

3 *The library*

Rejoice in the Lord always. I will say it again: Rejoice! Let
your gentleness be evident to all. The Lord is near. Do not
be anxious about anything, but in everything, by prayer
and petition, with thanksgiving, present your requests to

God. And the peace of God, which transcends all understanding, will guard your hearts and your minds in Christ Jesus.

Finally, brothers, whatever is true, whatever is noble, whatever is right, whatever is pure, whatever is lovely, whatever is admirable – if anything is excellent or praiseworthy – think about such things. Whatever you have learned or received or heard from me, or seen in me – put it into practice. And the God of peace will be with you.

I rejoice greatly in the Lord that at last you have renewed your concern for me. Indeed, you have been concerned, but you had no opportunity to show it. I am not saying this because I am in need, for I have learned to be content whatever the circumstances. I know what it is to be in need, and I know what it is to have plenty. I have learned the secret of being content in any and every situation, whether well fed or hungry, whether living in plenty or in want. I can do everything through him who gives me strength.

Philippians 4: 4–13

4 *The music room*

Shout for joy to the Lord, all the earth.
  Serve the Lord with gladness;
  come before him with joyful songs.
Know that the Lord is God.
  It is he who made us, and we are his;
  we are his people, the sheep of his pasture.

Enter his gates with thanksgiving
  and his courts with praise;
  give thanks to him and praise his name.
For the Lord is good and his love endures for ever;
  his faithfulness continues
    through all generations.

Psalm 100

5 *The quiet room*

We prisoners have experienced the power of God, the love of God which made us leap with joy. Prison has

proved that love is as strong as death. We have conquered through Christ. Officers with rubber truncheons
came to interrogate us; we interrogated them, and they
became Christians. Other prisoners had been converted
. . . The Communists believe that happiness comes from
material satisfaction; but alone in my cell, cold, hungry
and in rags, *I danced for joy every night* . . . Sometimes I
was *so filled with joy* that I felt I would burst if I did not give
it expression . . . I had discovered a beauty in Christ
which I had not known before.

Pastor Richard Wurmbrand, *In God's Underground,*
W. H. Allen

Let us fix our eyes on Jesus,

*   *   *   *

– who for the *joy* set before him endured the cross, scorning its shame, and sat down at the right hand of the
throne of God.
CONSIDER HIM –

*   *   *   *

– who endured such opposition from sinful men, so that
you will not grow weary and lose heart.

Hebrews 12: 2f

Lord Jesus Christ, may we fix our eyes on you today, and
catch some of your joy.

May we always turn in every situation to consider you, so
that we never grow weary or lose heart.

We ask it in your name.   Amen.

6 *The living room*

Many different sounds are heard in our living room! Sound
is a gift from God. It is a means by which God communicates with man, man with God and man with man. But like
all God's gifts, sound can be abused. Man expresses his
feelings and desires, his freedom and frustrations, his love
and hate, his joy and sorrow, his dis-ease and wholeness by
the use of sound.

Man uses sound to reveal the fulness and depths of his being and also to hide his emptiness and loneliness. He uses it to express all that is good and all that is evil; all that is health-giving and all that is health-depriving. As sound is a gift of God, we must give thanks to the Giver. As it is abused, it must be redeemed by Jesus Christ.

> Lord, our heavenly Father,
>   we pray that your kingdom will come
>   on earth as in heaven,
>   when the sound of war
>   will become the sound of peace;
>   the sound of discord –
>   the sound of harmony;
>   the sound of weeping –
>   the sound of joy;
>   the sound of bitterness –
>   the sound of sweetness;
>   the sound of breaking –
>   the sound of unity;
>   the sound of pain –
>   the sound of healing;
>   the sound of evil –
>   the sound of the kingdom;
>   and the sound of men
>   will become the voice of Christ,
>   our Lord and Saviour.   Amen.
>   Fred Belcher

7 *The door into the world*

> Praise the Lord.
> Praise God in his sanctuary;
>   praise him in his mighty heavens.
> Praise him for his acts of power;
>   praise him for his surpassing greatness.
> Praise him with the sounding of the trumpet,
>   praise him with the harp and lyre,
> praise him with tambourine and dancing,
>   praise him with the strings and flute,
> praise him with the clash of cymbals,

praise him with resounding cymbals.

Let everything that has breath
  praise the lord.

Praise the Lord.

Psalm 150

Those who bring sunshine to the lives of others cannot keep it from themselves.

James M. Barrie

It is good if man can bring about that God sings within him.

Rabbi Elimelekh, HBCQ

May the God of hope *fill us with all joy* and peace as we put our trust in him, so that we may overflow with hope by the power of the Holy Spirit;
and may the blessing of God Almighty, Father, Son and Holy Spirit, be upon us and remain with us always. Amen.

Romans 15: 13

DAY 19

LET GO, LET GOD

1 *The entrance to the house of God's glory*

> Sing to the Lord a new song;
> sing to the Lord, all the earth.
> Sing to the Lord, praise his name;
> proclaim his salvation day after day.
>
> Psalm 96: 1

If you will you can be cured. Deliver yourself to the physician, and he will cure the eyes of your soul and heart.
Who is the physician? He is God, who heals and gives life through the Word and wisdom.

> St Theophilus of Antioch (to Autolycus) Book 1, 2, 7

> Let nothing perturb you, nothing frighten you.
> All things pass;
> God does not change.
> Patience achieves everything.
> Whoever has God lacks nothing.
> God alone suffices.
>
> St Teresa (found in her breviary after her death)

2 *The therapy room*

> O Blessed Jesus, my Master and my Friend teach
>   me Thy way of living;
> Teach me to know, deeply in my inmost being that
>   God my Father is sustaining me;

Teach me to know, without shadow of doubt, that
   His love is fixed on me, and faileth not;
Teach me that that great love is healing me, and
   renewing every corner of my being;
Teach me, Good Master, that my heavenly Father
   knows all my needs, and is fulfilling them now;
Teach me that my body is an abiding place of Thy
   Holy Spirit, and that His Light is shining in me
   more and more unto the day of my perfecting;
Teach me, Good Lord, that I am ever in Thee, and
   Thou in me, and that I shall lack no manner of
   thing that is good.
And teach me, Thou Chief of Ministers, to minister
   also myself as far as in me lies, to the wants of
   other folk round me, and do it willingly and
   cheerfully, that seeing Thee in them, I may thus
   minister unto Thee.   Amen.

William Portsmouth, Healing Prayer, p 83,
Arthur James 1954

3 *The library*

I have seen many a depressed person's healing begin as
we quieten ourselves in His Presence and ask Him to
bring up the deepest desire of the heart, that one the
sufferer has been too fearful ever to acknowledge before.
Then conversation with God about it begins. It takes the
real self truly to desire, and in its desiring all that is good,
beautiful and true, it more quickly and wonderfully
functions in the image of its Maker.

In listening prayer we gain the hallowed space and
time needed to befriend our emotions, those jaded or
stunted in the past, or those feared and rejected and
therefore repressed. Our emotions of anger, grief, joy,
love, and shame, along with deeply repressed desires of
our hearts, are brought into this holy converse with God.
In His loving acceptance, our emotional being grows
into a delicate and gentle balance with our sensory and
intellectual being. We need no longer be shaped by our
emotional needs and deprivations, but rather will see
them healed.

In this converse with God, for the moment we have opened as widely as we can our hearts to the Lord. He has known all along what was there and what was needed. Now our *wills* are one with His, and we have consented to yield up to Him what has heretofore been garnered in our hearts. We are now ready for that most important moment in prayer. True prayer is, like all else that partakes of the *Real*, incarnational; that is, it is a reception of God's life. We ask Him to come in more fully, and to fill all the spaces of our being (especially those we have just emptied) with Himself. This is the moment for 'letting that other larger, stronger, quieter life come flowing in . . . We can do it only for moments at first. But from those moments the new sort of life will be spreading through our systems because now we are letting Him work at the right part of us.'

Leanne Payne, *The Broken Image*, Crossway Books,
Westchester, Illinois 1981
The quotation at the end is from C. S. Lewis, *Mere Christianity*

4 *The music room*

God is Love: let heav'n adore him;
    God is Love: let earth rejoice;
Let creation sing before him,
    and exalt him with one voice.
He who laid the earth's foundation,
    he who spread the heav'ns above,
He who breathes through all creation,
    he is Love, eternal Love.

God is Love: and he enfoldeth
    all the world in one embrace;
With unfailing grasp he holdeth
    every child of every race.
And when human hearts are breaking
    under sorrow's iron rod,
Then they find that selfsame aching
    deep within the heart of God.

God is Love: and though with blindness
    sin afflicts the souls of men,

God's eternal loving-kindness
  holds and guides them even then.
Sin and death and hell shall never
  o'er us final triumph gain;
God is love, so Love for ever
  o'er the universe must reign.
Timothy Rees (1874–1939)

In HFT 32 this is set to the tune 'Alleluia' with the alternative 'Hyfrydol'.

5 The quiet room

God is at work at the point where my difficulties are occurring. He is Power and Health, so He is trying to overcome disease. He is Love and Serenity, so He is trying to quieten my troubled mind. He is Purpose and Plan, so He is trying to direct my will and guide me into His way.

I here and now affirm my readiness to submit to Him and to co-operate with Him, and I honestly pray to be shown where I am standing in His way and defeating Him, or where others are doing so.

I will accept only the evil which cannot be altered, and then I know He will weave that, however different from His ideal will, into His pattern of ultimate good.

Leslie Weatherhead, A Private House of Prayer

A moment's quiet while we allow God to work his healing deep within us.
Let go – *let God*.

6 The living room

For the morning:
Dear Lord and Father, in my need I turn to Thee to pray that Thy Holy Spirit, Who is in me now, may increase in me more and more, filling every part of me until my soul and mind and body show forth the Light of Thy glory. I trust myself to Thy sufficiency, knowing that Thou art

working in me for good. Enable me to go on trusting in Thy healing grace. Grant that nothing that may happen today may shake that trust, but help me in every event to cling surely to the knowledge that Thou art with me. I thank Thee, Father, that Thou hast heard me. I thank Thee, Jesus, that Thy Spirit of Life and Light is in me now to heal.   Amen.

For the evening:
In the stillness of the evening, O Father God, I would still my mind and heart, to become aware of Thy all-pervading Presence; I would cast out of me all the warring emotions, all the fiery darts of evil within, all the disharmony, all the poisons which disturb the mind. And I would become increasingly conscious of the reality of Thy Peace round me and in me. I would close my eyes to all outward things, and know the only Truth, Thyself, dwelling within me, giving me harmony, unity, and the strength of Thy peace.   Amen.

William Portsmouth, *Healing Prayer*, pp 65, 129,
Arthur James 1954

7 *The door into the world*

Do not worry, saying, 'What shall we eat?' or 'What shall we drink?' or 'What shall we wear?' For the pagans run after all these things, and your heavenly Father knows that you need them. But seek first his kingdom and his righteousness, and all these things will be given to you as well. Therefore do not worry . . .

Matthew 6: 31–34

Lord, teach us this day and every day to trust you for everything, to *let go and let God*; may we commit into your keeping our problems and burdens and allow you to come and take control of every situation, as did the Apostles. They prayed, *Lord, consider their threats*, committing to you their whole anxiety of not being able to proclaim your gospel; they got out of the way in order that you alone would show them the way.

Lord, as they did, we too ask for *boldness*, born of an inner conviction that you are in charge, that you reign in the universe; so shall we see the *signs and wonders* that will follow *through the name of your holy servant Jesus.* Amen.

God be in my head, and in my understanding;
God be in my eyes, and in my looking;
God be in my mouth, and in my speaking;
God be in my heart, and in my thinking;
God be at my end, and at my departing. Amen.

Pynson's *Horae*, 1515, AMR 332

DAY 20

MATURE PERSONHOOD

1 *The entrance to the house of God's glory*

Like newborn babies, crave pure spiritual milk, so that by
it you may grow up in your salvation, now that you have
tasted that the Lord is good.

1 Peter 2: 2, 3

. . . so that the body of Christ may be built up until we all
reach unity in the faith and in the knowledge of the Son of
God and become mature, attaining to the whole measure
of the fulness of Christ.

Ephesians 4: 12, 13

Many of us do not grow in inner health and maturity as
we grow in bodily health, mental ability and control over
outside things. Few of us devote to God and the study of
his will the same time and application that we give to
worldly studies and professional training. The writers
of the New Testament frequently lament the lack of
maturity in the Christians for whom they are writing.
That spiritual maturity is essential for inner health, right
attitudes and right decisions and is creative for a
dimension of life beyond the physical and the material.

George Appleton, *Journey for a Soul*, Collins, Fontana 1974

O God, I recognize that my sins are spiritual sickness,
selfishness, incompleteness, immaturity, falling short of
your will and your glory. Let your grace heal me, make
me selfless, lead me to maturity and holiness, complete

me, according to the pattern of your unique Son, Jesus
Christ, my Lord.   Amen.

ibid

2 *The therapy room*

Dr Martin Israel depicts the mature person in the following
way. How do I make out by comparison?

> Mature people are independent of the fads, fashions and
> prejudices of those around them. They lead individual
> lives, yet work harmoniously and efficiently with others.
> They know when to conform and when not to. They
> know how to avoid the polarities of collectivism and
> individualism. They take people for what they are in
> themselves, rather than for what their colour, race or
> class is. They have a sense of humour and are able to
> laugh at the vicissitudes and absurdities of life, including
> their own foibles. They can detect humbug and cant and
> are merely amused by pomposity and self-importance.
> They live in the moment and have an awareness of
> present things. They do not dwell on past regrets or
> future fears. They can communicate easily and so form
> deep relationships. Such people strike others as creative,
> harmonious, intelligent and understanding.

George Appleton, Journey for a Soul

I know that nothing good lives in me, that is, in my sinful
nature. For I have the desire to do what is good, but I
cannot carry it out. For what I do is not the good I want to
do; no, the evil I do not want to do – this I keep on doing.
Now if I do what I do not want to do, it is no longer I who
do it, but it is sin living in me that does it.

So I find this law at work: When I want to do good, evil
is right there with me. For in my inner being I delight in
God's law; but I see another law at work in the members
of my body, waging war against the law of my mind and
making me a prisoner of the law of sin at work within my
members. What a wretched man I am! Who will rescue
me from this body of death? *Thanks be to God – through
Jesus Christ our Lord!*

Romans 7: 18–25

3 The library

Those who carry heavy responsibilities in a community must look at their own interior life: are they blotting it out, or dispersing it in activity, or are they trying to nurture it? It is too easy to live on the periphery of ourselves, using our superficial energies instead of constantly working to deepen our interiority and our contact with the silent places at our heart where God lives.

The more we become people of action and responsibility in our community, the more we must become people of contemplation. If we do not nurture our deep emotional life in prayer hidden in God, if we do not spend time in silence, if we do not know how to take time to live from the presence and gentleness of our brothers and sisters, we risk becoming embittered. It is only to the extent that we nurture our own hearts that we can keep interior freedom. People who are hyperactive, fleeing from their deep selves and their wound, become tyrannical and their exercise of responsibility becomes intolerable, creating nothing but conflict . . .

We all carry our own deep wound, which is the wound of our loneliness. We find it hard to be alone, and we try to flee from this in hyperactivity, through television and in a million other ways. Some people think their wound of loneliness will be healed if they come into community. But they will be disappointed. While they are young, they can hide their disappointment behind the dynamic of generosity; they can flee from the present by projecting themselves into the future, into a hope that things will be better tomorrow. But towards the age of forty, the future is past and there are no more great projects; the wound is still there and we can become depressed, especially as we are now carrying all the guilt and apathy of the past. Then we have to realise that this wound is inherent in the human condition and that what we have to do is walk with it instead of fleeing from it. We cannot accept it until we discover that we are loved by God just as we are, and that the Holy Spirit, in a mysterious way, is living at the centre of the wound . . .

If the Spirit has called people to make the first passage from the discovery of new horizons (the time of adolescence) to determination and choice in a community, he will guide them in their *journey towards maturity* and wisdom and help them grow at all times. But if the first passage is made at high noon, under a shining sun, often surrounded by friends, the second – that of renunciation – is often made at night. We feel alone and we are afraid because we are entering a world of confusion. We begin to doubt the commitment we made in the heat of the day. We seem deeply broken in some ways. But this suffering is not useless. Through the renunciation we can reach a new wisdom of love . . .

Old age is the most precious time of life, the one nearest eternity. There are two ways of growing old. There are old people who are anxious and bitter, living in the past and illusion, who criticize everything that goes on around them. Young people are repulsed by them; they are shut away in their sadness and loneliness, shrivelled up in themselves. But there are also old people with a child's heart, who have used their freedom from function and responsibility to find a new youth. They have the wonder of a child, but *the wisdom of maturity* as well. They have integrated their years of function and so can live without being attached to power. Their freedom of heart and their acceptance of their limitations and weakness make them people whose radiance illuminates the whole community. They are gentle and merciful, symbols of compassion and forgiveness. They become a community's hidden treasures, sources of unity and life.

Jean Varnier, *Community and Growth*,
Darton, Longman & Todd 1979

4 *The music room*

O God, in this thine hour of grace,
　With needy heart and empty hand,
Yet bidden of thee to seek thy face,
　For blessing at thy feet we stand.

Ours are the vows, the frail desires,
　The high resolve to dare and do;
Our flickering faith to thee aspires,
　And passes like the morning dew.

Ours is the mighty need of thee –
How great, thy love alone can know;
Ours but the hunger and the plea
That strives and will not let thee go.

Thy word we clasp, thy touch we wait;
Our eyes, O God, are unto thee,
Whose lovingkindness makes us great,
Whose strength shall seal our victory.
C. H. Boutflower, AMR 460

5 The quiet room

I want to know Christ and the power of his resurrection
and the fellowship of sharing in his sufferings, becoming
like him in his death, and so, somehow, to attain to the
resurrection from the dead.

Not that I have already obtained all this, or have
already been made perfect, but I press on to take hold of
that for which Christ Jesus took hold of me. Brothers, I do
not consider myself yet to have taken hold of it. But one
thing I do: Forgetting what is behind and straining towards what is ahead, I press on towards the goal to win
the prize for which God has called me heavenwards in
Christ Jesus.

All of us who are mature should take such a view of
things.

Philippians 3: 10–15a

For Paul, the 'mature view of things' had to do with the
pressing on 'towards the goal' of his calling, being moved
on towards an ever deeper knowledge of God in Christ by
the Holy Spirit of Movement.

This entailed – 1 'Forgetting what is behind'. The road to
health and maturity involves ceasing to dwell on past
wounds – the hurts and resentments, the failures and
defeats – which we all have experienced. The medicine for
this was –

2 'straining towards what is ahead', like an athlete who
looks only at the track in front of him and the finishing tape.
God's call to him 'heavenwards' is his motivation to win the
prize and gain a more mature perspective on life.

What luggage from my past life needs to be left behind?

* * * *

Where do I need to make progress (= the forward move to maturity) in the Christian life?

* * * *

Let us fix our eyes on Jesus, the author and perfecter of our faith, who for the joy set before him endured the cross, scorning its shame, and sat down at the right hand of the throne of God.

Hebrews 12: 2

6 *The living room*

Rejoice in the Lord always. I will say it again: Rejoice! Let your gentleness be evident to all. The Lord is near. Do not be anxious about anything, but in everything, by prayer and petition, with thanksgiving, present your requests to God.

Philippians 4: 4, 5, 6

Lord, I truly want to present my requests before
    you today with joy and thanksgiving.
I ask that you will anoint me with deep joy,
  joy that will be matched by a thankful heart,
  joy that wells up in the knowledge of sins
      forgiven,
  joy that always rejoices, even in life's crosses,
    because it is the gift of your resurrection,
    because you are at hand.
With thanksgiving for all, I ask you to anoint,
    with that same inward joy –
  all for whom I have a care this day . . .
  all who pray for me this day . . .
  all who minister in any way
    to those who are full of cares and anxieties,
    to those who are sick or infirm this day . . .
Give them all the joy of knowing you are at hand.
    And let us all have space to rejoice this day,
      space to hear the song of birds,

the laughter of children,
the silence of your Presence,
and opportunity to smile at others.
So enable us to be joyful and thankful
as we offer you our prayers and supplications.
And the peace of God shall keep our hearts and
minds in Christ Jesus. Amen.

7 *The door into the world*

You, however, are controlled not by the sinful nature but
by the Spirit, if the Spirit of God lives in you. And if
anyone does not have the Spirit of Christ, he does not
belong to Christ. But if Christ is in you, your body is dead
because of sin, yet your spirit is alive because of righteousness. And if the Spirit of him who raised Jesus from
the dead is living in you, he who raised Christ from the
dead will also give life to your mortal bodies through his
Spirit, who lives in you . . . For you did not receive a
spirit that makes you a slave again to fear, but you
received the Spirit of sonship. And by him we cry, '*Abba*,
Father.' The Spirit himself testifies with our spirit that we
are God's children. Now if we are children, then we are
heirs – heirs of God and co-heirs with Christ, if indeed we
share in his sufferings in order that we may also share in
his glory.

Romans 8: 9–11, 15–17

Only when the Spirit of God takes possession of the 'old'
man to transform him is the man made whole again. It is
only when this threshold is crossed that personality takes
on full meaning and significance.

Emile Cailliet, HBCQ p124

May God himself, the God of peace, sanctify us through
and through. May our whole spirit, soul and body be
kept blameless at the coming of our Lord Jesus Christ, for
the one who calls us is faithful and he will do it. Amen.

1 Thessalonians 5: 23, 24

DAY 21

PEACE

1 *The entrance to the house of God's glory*

Suddenly a great company of the heavenly host appeared
with the angel, praising God and saying,
  'Glory to God in the highest,
  and on earth peace to men
  on whom his favour rests.'

Luke 2: 13, 14

On the evening of that first day of the week, when the
disciples were together, with the doors locked for fear of
the Jews, Jesus came and stood among them and said,
'Peace be with you!'

John 20: 19

When Christ came into the world, peace was sung; and
when he went out of the world, peace was bequeathed.

Francis Bacon

Holy Spirit, I offer myself to your work of healing, peace
and reconciliation. In my busy world bless my silent
moments. In the stillness of my heart may I find peace
within myself, peace with others, and peace with
you. Amen.

Michael Buckley

2 *The therapy room*

O Spirit of God, set at rest the crowded, hurrying,
anxious thoughts within our hearts and minds.

Let the peace and quiet of Thy presence take possession of us. Help us to rest, to relax, to become open
and receptive to Thee. Thou dost know our innermost
spirits, the hidden unconscious life within us, the forgotten memories of hurts and fears, the frustrated desires, the unresolved tensions and dilemmas. Cleanse
and sweeten the springs of our being, that freedom, life
and love may flow both into our conscious and hidden
life. Lord we lie open before Thee, waiting for Thy peace,
Thy healing and Thy word.   Amen.

George Appleton

3 The library

Peace was a word frequently found on Jesus' lips; it was
his first gift to his followers after his resurrection. Its
general sense is determined by the positive conception of
the Hebrew word *shalom*, which in the Old Testament
covers the idea of well-being in the widest sense of the
word – prosperity, bodily health, contentedness, good
relations between nations and men, salvation. It has
political connotations and a public significance far
beyond the purely personal. J. I. Durham contends that it
is often indicative 'of a comprehensive kind of fulfilment
or completion, indeed of a perfection in life and spirit
which quite transcends any success which man alone,
even under the best of circumstances, is able to attain'.
And again, '(*shalom*) is the gift of God, and can be
received only in his Presence.' Jesus's act on the first
Easter Day was therefore of supreme significance.

The state of *shalom* comes about when the will of God is
being done, when there is a harmony of being at one with
the purposes of the Creator, the popular symbol for
which was the ideal time when every man could sit under
his vine and fig tree. It is left to Jeremiah to discern that
true peace can come only through a radical change of
heart and the writing of a new covenant deep within (31:
33). One of the messianic titles was Prince of Peace (Isaiah
9:6) and so Jesus 'came and preached peace to you who
were far off and peace to those who were near' (Ephesians 2:17). It was peace that would involve suffering and

not yield to any easy solution: 'Do not think that I have come to bring peace on earth; I have not come to bring peace, but a sword' (Matthew 10:34/Luke 12:51). He pronounces 'Woes' on the Pharisees and drives out from the Temple those whose lives are set on selfish gain. But always one is left with the feeling that here is the Prince of Peace fighting for the ultimate good, the health and *shalom* of his people and his Father's creation. This is the supreme cause for which the Prince of Peace dies – the fullness and perfection of God's creation, the perfect time when God's Kingdom becomes creation healed. The peacemakers, those who follow the Prince in this work, are therefore accorded a special title and position: 'Blessed are the peacemakers, for they shall be called the Sons of God' (Matthew 5:9). To be a fellow son and heir with Christ is healing indeed, but we have to experience peace *with* God before we can know the peace *of* God.

M. M., *The Christian Healing Ministry*, pp 10f

4 *The music room*

We turn to you, O God of every nation,
    giver of life and origin of good;
your love is at the heart of all creation,
    your hurt is people's broken brotherhood.

We turn to you, that we may be forgiven
    for crucifying Christ on earth again.
We know that we have never wholly striven,
    forgetting self, to love the other man.

Free every heart from pride and self-reliance,
    our ways of thought inspire with simple grace;
break down among us barriers of defiance,
    speak to the soul of all the human race.

On men who fight on earth for right relations
    we pray the light of love from hour to hour.
Grant wisdom to the leaders of the nations,
    the gift of carefulness to those in power.

Teach us, good Lord, to serve the need of others,
    help us to give and not to count the cost.
Unite us all, for we are born as brothers:
    defeat our Babel with your Pentecost.
                                Fred Kaan (1929), HFT 189

5 The quiet room

I may now know the deep, illuminating Peace of union
with Thee, Most High within me.
    I would be healed of all that bears not the likeness of
Thy Love and Wisdom, Thy Joy and Beauty.
    Healed of all that is unloving, foolish, gloomy or ugly
in my emotional life, I shall be truly alive in Peace, for I
shall be in the state of fulfilment proper to me as a child of
God.

*   *   *   *

Our failure to meditate regularly, or our acquiescence in
negative states of emotion, or our mental subservience to
the transient is not simply an obstacle to our own personal development. Our eyes are opened and we discern
our negative states as stumbling blocks to others as well
as ourselves, something that may hinder them in their
pilgrimage to union with the Divine.

*   *   *   *

Remembering this, I affirm and now receive Thy Peace,
the deep illuminating Peace of union with Thee, Most
High within me.

*   *   *   *

Leslie Weatherhead, *A Private House of Prayer*, Hodder 1958

6 The living room

Father of peace and God of love, grant us your peace.

Send your peace to the world.
    Take from the world the threat of war, and bring in the
    time when the nations will live in friendship with

each other, united as subjects of that Kingdom of which you are King, and as members of that Family of which you are Father. Give us strength and grace, faith and courage to build a world in which there are no national barriers, no political divisions, no iron curtains, no dividing walls, no colour bar, but in which men are one in Jesus Christ.

Send your peace to our country.

In politics help men to set the state above the party, and to set your will above all else.

In industry take away all suspicion and distrust. Put into men's minds the pride of craftsmanship and the desire to be workmen who have never any need to be ashamed of their work. Make employers to see their responsibilities to their employees, and make employees to see their duty to their employers, that all may work in brotherhood together for the common good.

Send peace within ourselves.

Help us to live in peace with our fellow human beings. Rid us of the bitter and the unforgiving spirit. Control our temper and our tongue. Grant that we may nourish no grudge within our hearts and no memory of injury within our minds, and grant that love may banish hate.

Give us within our own hearts the peace that passes understanding.

Take from us the worries which distract us, and give us more trust.

Take from us the doubts which disturb us, and make us more sure of what we believe.

Take from us the wrong desires from which our temptations come, and make us more pure in heart.

Take from us the false ambitions which drive us, and make us more content to serve you where we are and as we are.

Take from us all estrangement from you and give us the peace of sins forgiven.

All this we ask through Jesus Christ our Lord.   Amen.

William Barclay, *Prayers for the Christian Year*, SCM Press 1964

7 *The door into the world*

Jesus said, Blessed are the peacemakers, for they will be
called sons of God.

Matthew 5: 9

> Send us forth alert and living,
> Sins forgiven, wrongs forgiving,
>   in your Spirit strong and free.
> Finding love in all creation,
> Bringing peace in every nation,
>   may we faithful followers be.
>
> H. C. A. Gaunt (1902–   ), HFT 83

The peace of God, which passes all understanding, keep
our hearts and minds in the knowledge and love of God,
and of his Son Jesus Christ our Lord, and may the
blessing of God almighty, the Father, the Son, and the
Holy Spirit, be among us and remain with us always.
Amen.

The Order for Holy Communion Rite B, ASB

DAY 22

PRAYER AND HEALING

1 *The entrance to the house of God's glory*

One day Jesus was praying in a certain place. When he finished, one of his disciples said to him, 'Lord, teach us to pray, just as John taught his disciples.'

Luke 11:1

There was a timeless quality about the life of Jesus. His earthly life was lived in the shadow of eternity. There were thirty years of virtual silence in preparation for three years of ministry. He invariably gave himself space. A long while before day he went out alone into the hills to commune with his heavenly Father. His life was lived in a contemplative stillness which allowed him to be a person of vision and realise his destiny. 'Crowds of people came to hear him and to be healed of their sicknesses. But Jesus often withdrew to lonely places and prayed' (Luke 5: 15–16). Not even the pressures and demands of real human need deflected him from his own spiritual journey.

M. M., Journey to Wholeness, pp 48f

Jesus said to them, 'When you pray, say:
"Father,
hallowed be your name,
your kingdom come.
Give us each day our daily bread.
Forgive us our sins,
for we also forgive everyone who
sins against us.
And lead us not into temptation."'

Luke 11: 2–4

2 *The therapy room*

The Christian therapist must inevitably be a person of prayer, daily exercising this channel to God. Faced with disease and disorder, be it physical, psychological or spiritual, he is then adequately armed. We are permitted to know some of the specific circumstances under which Jesus entered his 'inner chamber'. He did so just before choosing his disciples. He often resorted there before and after days crowded with labour, teaching and excitement. His forty days of temptations were preceded by days of prayer. And we think of the bloody sweat of Gethsemane and how even that place became an inner chamber of prayer and eventually of peace. Jesus always emerged from his inner chamber calm, strengthened and re-endued with heavenly power.

And what it was for him, the inner chamber has become again and again to his disciples. A child remarked to Principal Rainy, a famous Scottish theologian and a glowing Christian, that she believed that he went to heaven every night because he appeared so happy every day. Principal Rainy revealed his secret when he said, 'Joy is the flag which is flown from the castle of the heart when the King is in residence.' And what is true of joy, is true also of peace, love and life. The Christian therapist must be a person of the inner chamber, a person of prayer.

> Dr David Enoch, *Healing the Hurt Mind*, p 129

Thanks be to Thee, my Lord Jesus Christ,
   for all the blessings Thou hast given me,
   for all the pains and insults Thou hast borne for
     me,
O most merciful Redeemer, Friend and Brother,
   may I know Thee more clearly,
   love Thee more dearly,
   and follow Thee more nearly,
     day by day.   Amen.
> Prayer of St Richard of Chichester (1197–1253)

3 The library

I think that real prayer does not begin until after all the immediate needs of our souls are satisfied. When we come to God we are at first conscious of many needs, and not least our own pressing need for His forgiving and cleansing. His Spirit has to overcome such barriers in us before we can be at peace. As St Augustine said, 'Our hearts are restless till they rest in Thee'. Then there are all the thanksgivings we want to make for His mercies and the recollections of His grace at work in the lives of our loved ones and friends. Many voices press on us and have to die away. It takes time to enter into the deep places of prayer.

It is only when all these have passed and we begin to relax into His pervading presence that we enter fully into the world we call prayer. We can then begin to come into harmony with all creation and we find the sweet companionship of angelic beings and the smile of heaven. We listen as He speaks silently to us. Here we enter into an attunement with God in which souls are free. Here we find not so much a striving as an accepting: here there is no attempt to change the course of God's will but a joyful acceptance of it . . .

Prayer, whatever form it takes, is the greatest power in the world. Through prayer men are healed, saved, and born anew. In prayer we enter for awhile into the ceaseless movement of God's creative activity. In prayer we abide in the real but unseen world, for what is of significance in the world in which we live is but the outward expression of that which is within.

Prayer is not just the odd ten minutes or so we spend on our knees. It is a continuing conversation through each and every day. It is a continuing awareness of the movement of the Holy Spirit, especially in the lives of those we meet. Prayer is an aligning of our wills with the divine will, a uniting with Him as He seeks to bring His kingdom to us. Without prayer we begin to die.

Our Lord often told His disciples to pray. Five times in the intimacy of the Upper Room on the night He was betrayed, He encouraged them to bring their requests to the Father. 'Ask', He said, 'and you will receive, that your joy may be full.' . . .

Those three years of His earthly ministry have made a bigger impact on the whole course of history than any number of years in the life of any other man. And behind it all was prayer.

How did He pray? What method did He use? The questions seem almost pointless and impious. It was a simple abiding in the Father, a resting in the limitless resources of God's creative energies, a replenishing of divine power for His daily needs and for the needs of others. Prayer was His daily bread.

As He commissions us to continue His work, so does He know that it cannot be done in any other way than the way He did it. Without prayer there is no healing, for without prayer there is no life . . .

The heart of healing is found in prayer through which we come into the presence of the risen Christ and find our home in Him.

George Bennett, *The Heart of Healing*, Arthur James 1971

4 *The music room*

Today we 'sing' a prayer for the healing work to which we are called.

O God, by whose almighty plan
First order out of chaos stirred,
And life, progressive at your word,
Matured through nature up to man;
 Grant us in light and love to grow,
 Your sovereign truth to seek and know.

O Christ, whose touch unveiled the blind,
Whose presence warmed the lonely soul;
Your love made broken sinners whole,
Your faith cast devils from the mind.
 Grant us your faith, your love, your care
 To bring to sufferers everywhere.

O Holy Spirit, by whose grace
Our skills abide, our wisdom grows,

In every healing work disclose
New paths to probe, new thoughts to
trace.
    Grant us your wisest way to go
    In all we think, or speak, or do.
           H. C. A. Gaunt (1902–), HFT 73

5 *The quiet room*

Devote yourselves to prayer, being *watchful* and *thankful*.
                            Colossians 4: 2

*   *   *   *

The time I give to active work must be in proportion to what I give to the work of God, that is to prayer. I need more fervent and continual prayer to give character to my life. So I must give more time to meditation, and stay longer in the Lord's company, sometimes reading or saying my prayers aloud or just keeping silent. The company of Jesus will be my light, my comfort and my joy.
    Pope John XXIII, *Journal of a Soul*, Geoffrey Chapman 1964

More fervent and continual prayer –
More time to meditation –
Stay *longer* in the Lord's company –

*   *   *   *

Prayer is not only worship; it is also an invisible emanation of man's worshipping spirit – the most powerful form of energy that one can generate. The influence of prayer on the human mind and body is as demonstrable as that of secreting glands. Its results can be measured in terms of increased physical buoyancy, greater intellectual vigour, moral stamina, and a deeper understanding of the realities underlying human relationships.
                Alexis Carrel (1873–1944),
        scientist and Nobel prizewinner (1912)

*   *   *   *

Pray persistently about everything, and then you will
never do anything without God's help. (94)
Everything we say or do without prayer afterwards turns
out to be unreliable or harmful, and so shows us up
without our realizing it. (108)

St Mark the Ascetic (early fifth century),
Philokalia, vol. 1, pp 133f Faber 1979

* * * *

Devote yourselves to prayer, being watchful and thankful . . .

6 *The living room*

Lord, the one you love is sick. John 11:3
Mary and Martha sent a message to Jesus which was brief
and to the point. It was also entirely trustful: they knew
they could leave the welfare of their brother Lazarus safely
in the Lord's keeping. So they did not go into great detail
about the illness. They did not even ask him to call, though
doubtless they hoped he would. They were certain beyond
all doubt of Jesus' love and concern for their brother.

In the story (John 11: 1–44) Jesus was also confident. It is
recorded that he stayed *two more days* (v.6) before going to
see Lazarus. There is a right time, God's time, for a person
to be helped in trouble; and that assistance must be for the
glory of God.

We can learn from this trustfulness (of Mary and Martha
towards Jesus and of Jesus towards his heavenly Father)
when we pray for those who are sick. All that we need to
say is contained in that message to Jesus:
Lord, the one you love is sick.
We don't have to go into all the details and give the Lord our
diagnosis, let alone tell him what to do or offer him advice.
We know that his will for them is all they need and will be
worked out in life or death, in complete cure or sustaining
grace. We can surrender all anxiety we may have for them
as we surrender them unconditionally into his healing
hands. Let us do just that with those for whom we have a
burden today:
Lord, . . . you love is sick.
– and entrust them wholly to HIM.

* * * *

Lord, we thank you that you hear us, and we know you hear us always.   Amen.

7 The door into the world

We will give our attention to prayer and the ministry of the word.

Acts 6: 4

In 1905 James Moore Hickson, to whom the healing movement if we may call it such, owes much of its inspiration on a world scale, founded the Guild of Emmanuel (note the name), which was later to become the Divine Healing Mission. The Guild was to be a call to prayer, a call to Christian men and women to turn again to the healing Christ in giving themselves to prayer on behalf of the sick and needy. From the very beginning the healing movement has stood for a recalling of the Church to deep prayer. I believe that that initial emphasis on prayer is bearing fruit in this generation.

M. M., *Journey to Wholeness*, pp 76f

Christ our Healer, we ask you to bless the healing work of your Church, that it may fulfil your holy will and purpose;
Grant us, its members, the power to pray,
    and teach us to know and use all means of grace for the
    healing of your people according to your holy word:
    to those who minister and also to those who desire
        your healing, give true penitence, full pardon and
        perfect peace.
For you, Lord, are the Physician of Salvation and we ask for the sick the aid of your heavenly healing, for your Name's sake.   Amen.

Adapted from a prayer by Bishop T. H. Cashmore,
Prayers for Christian Healing, Mowbray 1958

May the Lord who heals fill us in every part with praise, this day and all our days.   Amen.

DAY 23

'PRESCRIPTION FOR ANXIETY'

1 *The entrance to the house of God's glory*

Jesus said, I tell you, *do not worry* about your life, what you will eat or drink; or about your body, what you will wear. Again he said, *Do not worry* about tomorrow, for tomorrow will worry about itself.

Matthew 6: 25, 34

Anxiety does not empty tomorrow of its sorrows, but only empties today of its strength.

Charles H. Spurgeon

Have mercy upon us, our Father, in those hours when the world seems empty of your presence, and no word comes to reassure our hearts; that in the darkness we may wait patiently for the light, and in the silence listen for your voice, and in all things trust your promises in Jesus Christ our Lord.   Amen.

New Every Morning, p 96, BBC 1974

A prayer of affirmation
>   The light of God surrounds me,
>   The love of God enfolds me,
>   The power of God protects me,
>   The presence of God watches over me,
>   Wherever I am, God is.

Catherine Marshall, *Something More*, p 253

2 *The therapy room*

O LORD, you have searched me
    and you know me.
You know when I sit and when I rise;
    you perceive my thoughts from afar.
You discern my going out and my lying down;
    you are familiar with all my ways.
Before a word is on my tongue
    you know it completely, O LORD.

You hem me in – behind and before;
    you have laid your hand upon me.
Such knowledge is too wonderful for me,
    too lofty for me to attain.

Where can I go from your Spirit?
    Where can I flee from your presence?
If I go up to the heavens, you are there,
    if I make my bed in the depths, you are there.
If I rise on the wings of the dawn,
    if I settle on the far side of the sea,
even there your hand will guide me,
    your right hand will hold me fast.

For you created my inmost being;
    you knit me together in my mother's womb.
I praise you because I am fearfully and wonderfully
    made;
    your works are wonderful,
    I know that full well.
My frame was not hidden from you
    when I was made in the secret place.
When I was woven together in the depths of the
    earth,
    your eyes saw my unformed body.
All the days ordained for me
    were written in your book
    before one of them came to be.

Search me, O God, and know my heart;
    test me and know my anxious thoughts.
See if there is any offensive way in me,
    and lead me in the way everlasting.

Psalm 139: 1–10, 13–16, 23, 24

3 *The library*

'Anxiety is such a ubiquitous and chronic ailment, that multitudes will thank God for sending to them through His servant this prescription for their malady.' This is what the great preacher James Stewart wrote about his friend Dr Leslie Weatherhead's book, *Prescription for Anxiety*, which provides the title of today's theme. Here Dr Weatherhead was suggesting four ways in which we can find help from the Christian religion:

1 Jesus looked away from himself to God. Even in His anguish He did that, and called God 'Father' at a time when it must have felt as though an omnipotent Father might have guided Him in a far less agonising path. In circumstances far less tragic, in the fret and turmoil of this age of anxiety, there must be continually for us times when we contemplate God, meditate upon Him and try to rest our fear-tossed minds in His greatness and adequacy . . . To look into the face of a primrose and meditate is to understand why Jesus talked as He did about the birds and the lilies. The calm contemplation of God in nature is a rebuke and remedy in our age of anxiety. 'Be not anxious', says Jesus, 'consider the lilies of the field.'

If we cannot get close to nature, we can contemplate God in His word. It would be a good thing for some of us to write out a few sentences from the Bible on a card and prop it up near our mirror, so that while we dress in the morning our minds can meditate on the themes they suggest:

'Be still and know that I am God.'
'The Lord God omnipotent reigneth.'
'The Lord is my Shepherd.'
'My peace I give unto you.'
'He is able to save to the uttermost.'
'The peace of God which passes understanding can
    stand sentry over our hearts and thoughts.'

Christ's message in an age of anxiety surely contains that direction. He Himself had no bogus security of money, no self-esteem that needed the bolstering of another's praise. (Anxiety is so often precipitated by an attack made on our self-esteem). He looked away to God and is saying to us something like this: 'Your Father knows. He understands and cares. He has got your situation in hand. He will tell you what to do. He is the Lord of history, the Master of everything we call accident, the Weaver of all our sins and failures and sorrows into His indestructible plans, and He is the Victor over death.'

2 When fighting anxiety consider the value of thankfulness. I am sure it is part of Christ's message. Note how He Himself continually thanked God in what we must call anxious moments. He said, 'Father, I thank Thee that Thou heardest Me.' What a profound utterance! He makes an act of thanksgiving about the past at the moment when He desires to banish all doubt and fear about the future from His mind (John 11: 41). One could call it a thankful affirmation.

It is a good thing to begin each day thanking God for His many blessings in the past. Could any act be more likely to dispel anxiety feelings than to affirm thankfully what God has done for one in the past? For, clearly God has not changed, and we thus meet the present and face the future confident that He Who has seen us through in the past will stand by us now . . .

The very act of thanking God excludes the devastating and disintegrating devils of moaning and whining and grumbling and telling our grievances to all and sundry. Thankfulness, above all, eliminates the worst devil of all, self-pity. Let us search our hearts and make sure that in the premises of our personality there are no meetings being held of the 'Let's be sorry for me' society. That society has too many branches.

3 Consider the value of attempting some kind of service for others . . . For myself, I have often been shamed out of worry and anxiety by making myself go to help another – or try to do so – only to find that the other, so much worse than I, showed far greater courage with far less reason.

I remember how a woman who had grumbled a dozen times because her feet ached, was silenced when she visited another with radiant face and loving heart, who could move neither hands nor feet, who could not even turn her head without pain . . .

A doctor, who started a prayer circle amongst his patients . . . said, 'I noticed that when a woman with headache, giddiness and a dry throat, is asked to pray for a man with cancer, *she at once feels better herself.* She realises that she might have worse diseases, and starts to think about someone else's troubles rather than her own.' . . . How significant is the sentence, 'The Lord turned the captivity of Job *when he prayed for his friends.'* (Job 42: 10).

4 Note another step on the way to freedom from anxiety.

We must *say every day, 'Into Thy hands I commit my spirit.'* What a significant thing St Luke records of Jesus! 'I must go on My way today and tomorrow and the day following.' (13: 33). Jesus said that when He was under the threat of murder. Can we every morning make an offering of the day to God, seeking to know and trying to follow His guidance regarding what should be done and said that day? Can we 'live a day at a time'? Can we really begin to want *His* way and kill the accursed self-centredness, which even more than any outward factors, like noise or threat of war, produces anxiety?

There is real freedom in saying to oneself, 'This is what God wants me to do today', or even, 'This is what He wants me to do during the next hour'. If only we can feel that there is a stream of purpose running through our lives and that that stream is as irresistible as the tides, then we can lose our fussy self-importance by yielding ourselves utterly to that purpose, that will, that holy stream. If I am ill, I am still in His hands. If I fail, I am still within His loving purpose. The only real tragedy that can happen to man would be to be spurned by God, but because God is love, that can never happen . . . We have Christ as our assurance on that point. 'I will never leave you nor forsake you,' is His promise. We may often be frightened, but if we can feel ourselves always within the purposes of God, we shall find peace.

Leslie Weatherhead, *Prescription for Anxiety*, Hodder 1956: Arthur James 1985

4 *The music room*

St Patrick's Breastplate

This day God gives me
strength of high heaven,
sun and moon shining,
    flame in my hearth,
flashing of lightning,
wind in its swiftness,
deeps of the ocean,
    firmness of earth.

This day God sends me
strength as my steersman,
might to uphold me,
    wisdom as guide.
Your eyes are watchful,
your ears are listening,
your lips are speaking,
    friend at my side.

God's way is my way,
God's shield is round me,
God's host defends me,
    saving from ill.
Angels of heaven,
drive from me always
all that would harm me,
    stand by me still.

Rising, I thank you,
mighty and strong One,
King of creation,
    giver of rest,
firmly confessing
Threeness of Person,
Oneness of Godhead,
    Trinity blest.

Words, adapted from St Patrick's Breastplate (8th century) by
James Quinn SJ (1919–   ), HFT 183

A prayer of St Patrick

Christ be with me, Christ within me,
Christ behind me, Christ before me,

Christ beside me, Christ to win me,
Christ to comfort and restore me,
Christ beneath me, Christ above me,
Christ in quiet, Christ in danger,
Christ in hearts of all that love me,
Christ in mouth of friend and stranger.
Translated Mrs C. F. Alexander, AMR 162

5 The quiet room

Jesus said, 'Therefore I tell you, do not worry about your life, what you will eat or drink; or about your body, what you will wear. Is not life more important than food, and the body more important than clothes? Look at the birds of the air; they do not sow or reap or store away in barns, and yet your heavenly Father feeds them. Are you not much more valuable than they? Who of you by worrying can add a single hour to his life? . . . So do not worry, saying, 'What shall we eat?' or 'What shall we drink?' or 'What shall we wear?' For the pagans run after all these things, and your heavenly Father knows that you need them. But seek first his kingdom and his righteousness, and all these things will be given to you as well. Therefore do not worry about tomorrow, for tomorrow will worry about itself. Each day has enough trouble of its own.
Matthew 6: 25–27, 31–34

* * * *

Anxiety is not only a pain which we must ask God to assuage but also a weakness we must ask him to pardon – for he's told us to take no care for the morrow.
C. S. Lewis

* * * *

As the deer pants for streams of water,
so my soul pants for you, O God.
My soul thirsts for God, for the living God.
When can I go and meet with God?
My tears have been my food day and night,
while men say to me all day long,
'Where is your God?'

These things I remember as I pour out my soul:
    how I used to go with the multitude,
    leading the procession to the house of God,
    with shouts of joy and thanksgiving
        among the festive throng.
Why are you downcast, O my soul?
Why so disturbed within me?
Put your hope in God,
    for I will yet praise him,
    my Saviour and my God.

                                    Psalm 42: 1–6

6 *The living room*

As a physician, I have seen men, after all other therapy
had failed, lifted out of disease and melancholy by serene
effort of prayer.

            Alexis Carrel (1873–1944), Nobel prize-winner (1912)

Lord, comfort the sick, the hungry, the lonely and those
who are hurt and shut in on themselves, by your
presence in their hearts; use us to help them in a practical
way.

    Show us how to set about this and give us strength, tact
and compassion. Teach us how to be alongside them,
and how to share in their distress deeply in our prayer.
Make us open to them and give us courage to suffer with
them, and that in so doing we share with you in the
suffering of the world for we are your body on earth and
you work through us.   Amen.

        Michael Hollings and Etta Gullick, *The One Who Listens*,
                            McCrimmon Publishing Co. Ltd

                        *   *   *   *

Christ heals today in the same way as He healed in the
days of His earthly ministry, but now He uses our faith,
yours and mine.

                                    Jim Glennon

                Lord, when I am hungry
                Give me someone to feed;
                When I am thirsty
                Give water for their thirst.

When I am sad
Someone to lift from sorrow.
When burdens weigh upon me
Lay upon my shoulders the burden of my fellows.
  Lord, when I stand
Greatly in need of tenderness,
Give me someone who yearns for love.
May your will be my bread;
    your grace my strength;
    your love my resting place.   Amen.

SU

7 The door into the world

O Lord, do not rebuke me in your anger
  or discipline me in your wrath.
Be merciful to me, Lord, for I am faint;
  O Lord, heal me, for my bones are in agony.
My soul is in anguish.
  How long, O Lord, how long?

* * * *

The Lord has heard my cry for mercy;
  the Lord accepts my prayer.

Psalm 6: 1–3, 9

Father, give to us, and to all your people,
    in times of anxiety, serenity;
    in times of hardship, courage;
    in times of uncertainty, patience;
    and at all times a quiet trust
        in your wisdom and love,
            through Jesus Christ our Lord.   Amen.

New Every Morning, p 101, BBC

To him who is able to keep you from falling
and to present you before his glorious presence
without fault and with great joy –
to the only God our Saviour
be glory, majesty, power and authority,
through Jesus Christ our Lord,
before all ages, now and for evermore.   Amen.

Jude 24f

DAY 24

SILENCE AND SOLITUDE

1 *The entrance to the house of God's glory*

At daybreak Jesus went out to a solitary place.
Luke 4: 42

Be still, and know that I am God.
Psalm 46: 10

If chosen souls could never be alone,
In deep mid-silence, open-doored to God,
No greatness ever had been dreamed or done.
James Russell Lowell (1819–91)

Teach us, O God, that silent language which says all
things. Teach our souls to remain silent in thy presence:
that we may adore thee in the deeps of our being and
await all things from thee, whilst asking of thee nothing
but the accomplishment of thy will. Teach us to remain
quiet under thine action and produce in our souls that
deep and simple prayer which specifies nothing and
expresses everything.   Amen.
John Nicholas Grou, HBCP 360

2 *The therapy room*

Holy Spirit, why are we so afraid of silence? Why do we
fill our lives with talk, and people, and work, and action,
until we feel guilty if we sit still and do nothing? Because
we do not want to hear God, who often speaks through
dullness, emptiness, stillness, loneliness?

Make us brave enough to try. Amen.

Monica Furlong, *Prayers for Today*,
edited Norman Goodacre, Mowbrays 1972

O God, let me rise to the edges of time and
   open my life to your eternity;
let me run to the edges of space and
   gaze into your immensity;
let me climb through the barriers of sound and
   pass into your silence;
And then, in stillness and silence
   let me adore You,
     Who are Life – Light – Love –
     without beginning and without end,
     the Source – the Sustainer – the Restorer –
     the Purifier – of all that is;
     the Love who has bound earth to heaven
      by the beams of a cross;
     the Healer who has renewed a dying race
      by the blood of a chalice;
     the God who has taken man into your glory
      by the wounds of sacrifice;
God . . . God . . . God . . . Blessed be God
   Let me adore you. Amen.

Sister Ruth, SLG, OBP 1985

3 *The library*

In Thomas Merton's spiritual teaching, some physical solitude, exterior silence, and real recollection are necessary for anyone who wants to have a serious prayer life. But they are means to an end. Solitude is not an end in itself, as though shutting myself off from the world, stuffing myself inside my own mind and closing the door like a turtle could have value. The purpose that exterior solitude serves is not isolation but communion. We 'go into the desert' for love of God and to enter into deeper communion with him; this is the primary purpose of physical solitude whether for an hour of prayer or a lifetime of living as a hermit. The secondary purpose regards other people; we go 'into the desert' not to escape

them but to learn how to find them, not to get rid of being
responsible for them, but to find out how to help them
the most . . .

For this reason, 'solitude is as necessary for society as
silence is for language and air for the lungs and food for
the body.' Any society needs to provide sufficient solitude to develop the inner life of the persons who form
that society . . .

With no solitude and no silence, I lose myself, become
alienated from my true self, and so too from God and
from others, and even from nature. In solitude, I can,
with God's grace, overcome my alienation. I can let my
false self crack and crumble off, and I can painfully
discover in the silence of God who I really am. 'The Lord
is watching in the almond trees, over the fulfilment of his
words,' writes Merton, referring to Jeremiah 1: 11, and he
adds that whether there is noise or not, whether there be
voices in the field or not, whether the radio is going or
silent, whether the house is full of children or empty, 'the
almond tree brings forth her fruit in silence.'

Robert Faricy, *Praying*, SCM Press 1983

(The works of Thomas Merton to which he refers are, in this
order, *New Seeds of Contemplation*, *Seeds of Contemplation* and
No Man is an Island).

Lord, lift Thou me up,
Or come right down,
That I may be with Thee,
And Thou with me.   Amen.

Sylvia Lake, who 'used it in prayer with Frank, in those last
days of his life, when words faded and silence was more
meaningful.'

4 *The music room*

Dear Lord and Father of mankind,
Forgive our foolish ways!
Re-clothe us in our rightful mind,
In purer lives thy service find,
In deeper reverence praise.

In simple trust like theirs who heard,
  Beside the Syrian sea,
The gracious calling of the Lord,
Let us, like them, without a word
  Rise up and follow thee.

O Sabbath rest by Galilee!
  O calm of hills above,
Where Jesus knelt to share with thee
The silence of eternity,
  Interpreted by love!

Drop thy still dews of quietness,
  Till all our strivings cease;
Take from our souls the strain and stress,
And let our ordered lives confess
  The beauty of thy peace.

Breathe through the heats of our desire
  Thy coolness and thy balm;
Let sense be dumb, let flesh retire;
Speak through the earthquake, wind, and fire,
  O still small voice of calm!

J. G. Whittier (1807–92), EH 383

5 *The quiet room*

Silence enables us to be aware of God . . .

*   *   *   *

. . . to let mind and imagination dwell, upon his
  truth . . .

*   *   *   *

. . . to let prayer be listening before it is talking . . .

*   *   *   *

. . . and to discover our own selves.

*   *   *   *

There comes sometimes an interior silence in which the
soul discovers itself in a new dimension of energy and
peace, a dimension which the restless life can miss.

Michael Ramsey, *Be Still and Know*, p 83

* * * *

Silence is the environment of creativity,
the essential condition for letting-be,
the birthplace of love.
Martin Thornton, *Prayer, a New Encounter*, p 67

* * * *

O Sabbath rest by Galilee!
O calm of hills above,
Where Jesus knelt to share with thee
The silence of eternity,
Interpreted by love!
J. G. Whittier (1807–92)

* * * *

Let the remembrance of Jesus be united to your breathing
and then you will know the value of silence.
Ladder of Divine Ascent 27

* * * *

6 *The living room*

Deep and silent and cool as a broad, still,
tree-shaded river
Is the peace of thy presence, thou rest of our souls.
From the thousand problems of this our hurrying
life
We turn, with silent joy, to plunge in thee,
To steep our souls in thy quiet depths
Where no clamour of earth disturbs our perfect
content.
Thou art our home and refuge;
In thee we are safe and at peace:
Even in the din and hurry of the world
We know that thou art near,
We know that close at hand – closer than our little
life –
Floweth that silent river of thy presence and love.
In a moment we may be with thee and in thee,
In a moment be surrounded and soaked in thy
peace:

In a moment, as this loud world clangs round us,
We may rest secure in the bliss of thine
    eternity.   Amen.

John S. Hoyland, HBCP 981

We bring to thee, O loving Saviour, those sufferers of
whom we think and whom we name in the silence of our
hearts . . . Forgive and remove everything in us which
spoils our prayers and prevents them from being channels of thy healing and comforting grace. As men and
women brought the sick to thee long years ago, we would
bring them through prayer and set them before thee. All
healing is with thee. We can only bring them to thee and
offer our minds in love and tenderness and sincerity.
Grant them healing if that may be, but, above all, grant
them thy peace and thy joy that they may know that thou
art with them, that they are safe and that nothing can
snatch them from thy hand or finally defeat thy purposes.
    We ask it for thy name's sake.   Amen.

Leslie Weatherhead, *A Private House of Prayer*

7 *The door into the world*

We need to find God, and he cannot be found in noise
and restlessness. God is the friend of silence. See how
nature – trees, flowers, grass – grows in silence. The more
we receive in prayer the more we can give in the active
life. We need silence to be able to touch souls. The
essential thing is not what we say but what God says
through us.

Mother Teresa of Calcutta

Then a great and powerful wind tore the mountains apart
and shattered the rocks before the Lord, but the Lord was
not in the wind. After the wind there was an earthquake,
but the Lord was not in the earthquake. After the earthquake came a fire, but the Lord was not in the fire. And
after the fire came a gentle whisper. When Elijah heard
it . . .

1 Kings 19: 11–13

Set a guard over my mouth, O Lord;
keep watch over the door of my lips.

Psalm 141: 3

The peace of God, which passes all understanding, keep
our hearts and minds in the knowledge and love of God,
and of his Son Jesus Christ our Lord: and the blessing of
God Almighty, the Father, the Son, and the Holy Spirit,
be among *us* and remain with *us* always.   Amen.

The blessing after Holy Communion, BCP/ASB

DAY 25

SPIRITUAL GROWTH

1 *The entrance to the house of God's glory*

I waited patiently for the LORD;
    he turned to me and heard my cry.
He lifted me out of the slimy pit,
    out of the mud and mire;
he set my feet on a rock
    and gave me a firm place to stand.
He put a new song in my mouth,
    a hymn of praise to our God.
Many will see and fear
    and put their trust in the LORD.

Psalm 40: 1–3

It is right that you should begin again every day. There is
no better way to finish the spiritual life than to be ever
beginning it over again, and never to think that you have
done enough.

St Francis de Sales

The glory of life
    is to love, not to be loved;
To serve, not to be served;
To be a strong hand in the dark
    to another in the time of need;
To be a cup of strength to any soul
    in a crisis of weakness;
To be a sound of beautiful music
    in the valleys of life:
This is to know
      THE GLORY OF LIFE.

SU

Lord, let me grow
and know *your* glory
in my life
and in the lives of others.   Amen.

2 *The therapy room*

Helper of men who turn to you,
Light of men in the dark,
Creator of all that grows from seed,
Promoter of all spiritual growth,
have mercy, Lord, on me
and make me a temple fit for yourself.
Do not scan my transgressions too closely,
for if you are quick to notice my offences,
I shall not dare to appear before you.
In your great mercy,
in your boundless compassion,
wash away my sins, through Jesus Christ,
your only Child, the truly holy,
the chief of our soul's healers,
Through him may all glory be given you,
all power and honour and praise,
throughout the unending succession of
ages.   Amen.

From a second-century papyrus, HBCP 396

3 *The library*

The *individuation* process is the name given by Jung to a
movement of maturing, which begins at birth or perhaps
even earlier in the pre-natal life of the infant. It is an
element in human growth and development . . . The
believer will see the movement towards individuation as
one of the ways by which the Creator guides men and
women towards their fulfilment. Jung has many illuminating observations about the stages which we pass
through in the journey from the cradle to the grave.
Reflection on these stages can help to make real the
presence of God throughout the whole of life . . .

Jung sees the individual's life as divided into four main stages which might be termed childhood, youth, maturity and old age. The first two stages belong to life's dawn and morning, the last two to its afternoon and evening. It is the two long middle periods which particularly interest Jung, for life is then full of problems which as a doctor he wants to help people solve. On the subject of youth's problems Jung writes:

> If we try to extract the common and essential factors from the almost inexhaustible variety of individual problems found in the period of youth, we meet in nearly all cases with a particular feature: a more or less patent clinging to the childhood level of consciousness – a rebellion against the fateful forces in and around us which tend to involve us in the world. Something in us wishes to remain a child; to be unconscious, or, at most, only conscious of the ego; to reject everything foreign, or at least subject it to our will; to do nothing, or else indulge our own craving for pleasure or power.

At this stage the individual's progress is best made by concentrating on one of the possibilities which invite him and developing that successfully. This will mean neglecting other possibilities at least for a time. A person with some artistic ability may have to give up painting in order to earn his living in a bank or in accountancy. Sometimes an individual must 'scorn delights and live laborious days' if he is to gain a footing in the world of adult achievement. To restrict ourselves to the attainable and to neglect the ideal, however valid as a temporary measure, is never a lasting solution to our problems. Much of Jung's work as a doctor and psychotherapist consisted in helping people who had sacrificed too much of themselves in the struggle for success at this stage of early adulthood. All the same Jung insists on the necessity for this struggle and its importance for the individual . . .

(Jung) likens human growth as we have seen to the course of a sun endowed with human feelings and man's limited consciousness. In the morning the sun rises from the night of unconsciousness and spreads its light and warmth over more and more of the world as it rises higher and higher in the sky. Then, at the stroke of noon the sun begins to descend. This descent means the reversal of the aims, values and ideals of the morning. Jung insists that the image of the rising and setting sun is not mere sentimental fairy-story. There is something sun-like within us, and to speak of the morning and evening, of the spring and autumn of life gives expression to psychological truths and even physiological facts. (He continues:)

> We cannot live the afternoon of life according to the programme of life's morning; for what was great in the morning will be little in the evening, and what in the morning was true will at evening have become a lie . . . Ageing people should know that their lives are not mounting or expanding, but that an inexorable inner process enforces the contraction of life. For a young person it is almost a sin, or at least a danger, to be too preoccupied with himself. After having lavished its light upon the world, the sun withdraws its rays in order to illuminate itself. Instead of doing likewise, many old people prefer to be hypochondriacs, niggards, pedants, applauders of the past or else eternal adolescents – all lamentable substitutes for the illumination of the self, but inevitable consequences of the delusion that the second half of life must be governed by the principles of the first.

Jung was convinced that the second half of life must have its own significance for the human species and should not be seen as a mere appendix to the pursuits and interests of the first half. Otherwise men and women would not go on living to seventy or eighty. The meaning of the second half of life is to be found in the service of culture in the broadest sense of the word. Culture then would include not only the arts – painting, sculpture, architecture, music and literature – but everything that broadens the mind and uplifts the spirit, everything that gives a transcendent meaning to life and especially religion . . . He points out that all the great religions promise a life beyond this life, and that this hope enables people to live in the second half of life with as much purpose and perseverance as in the first. (This gives people desire to live right up to the end with the courage and serenity proper to man.)

Christopher Bryant SSJE, *Jung and the Christian Way*,
Darton, Longman & Todd 1983

4 *The music room*

FILL thou my life, O Lord my God,
   In every part with praise,
That my whole being may proclaim
   Thy being and thy ways.

Not for the lip of praise alone,
   Nor e'en the praising heart,
I ask, but for a life made up
   Of praise in every part:

Praise in the common things of life,
   Its goings out and in;
Praise in each duty and each deed,
   However small and mean.

Fill every part of me with praise:
   Let all my being speak
Of thee and of thy love, O Lord,
   Poor though I be and weak.

So shalt thou, Lord, receive from me
   The praise and glory due;
And so shall I begin on earth
   The song for ever new.

So shall each fear, each fret, each care,
   Be turnèd into song;
And every winding of the way
   The echo shall prolong.

So shall no part of day or night
   Unblest or common be;
But all my life, in every step,
   Be fellowship with thee.

H. Bonar (1808–1889), AMR 373

5 *The quiet room*

Growth begins when we start to accept our own weakness.

* * * *

True growth comes from God, when we cry to him from the depths of the abyss to let his Spirit penetrate us. Growth in love is a growth in the Spirit.

* * * *

To grow in love is to allow this spirit of Jesus to grow in us. Growth takes on another dimension when we allow Jesus to penetrate us, to give us new life and new energy.

* * * *

It seems to me more and more that growth in the Holy Spirit brings us from a state of dreaming – and often illusion – to a state of realism.

* * * *

In his letter to Galatians, St Paul says that growth in love is growth in joy and patience, goodness, generosity, fidelity, tenderness and self-control. It is the opposite of all our tendencies to division.

* * * *

Perhaps the essential quality for anyone who lives in community is patience: a recognition that we, others, and the whole community take time to grow. Nothing is achieved in a day. If we are to live in community, we have to be friends of time.

* * * *

Each member of a community who grows in love and wisdom helps the growth of the whole community. Each person who refuses to grow, or is afraid to go forward, inhibits the community's growth. All the members of a community are responsible for their own growth and that of the community as a whole.

* * * *

I do not know if it is possible for any of us to grow without opening our heart to a witness to whom we have revealed the call of God for us and the small steps which he asks us to take. It is important from time to time to evaluate with this witness whether we are on the right road and, if not, how we are to refind our way.

Jean Vanier, *Community and Growth*,
Darton, Longman & Todd 1979

6 *The living room*

Today we shall pray for ourselves, as we ask the heavenly Father for grace to grow up into Christ through the power of the life-giving Spirit:

> Living and true God,
> You made us, you know us,
> you love us immensely, you are in us,
> guiding, guarding,
> helping, healing,
> cleansing, liberating.
> Open our hearts to you,
> that we may know you, trust you,
> and love you more and more.   Amen.
> A prayer used by Father Christopher Bryant,
> SSJE, at his workshops

> Father,
> I abandon myself into your hands;
> do with me what you will.
> Whatever you may do, I thank you;
> I am ready for all, I accept all.
> Let only your will be done in me,
> and in all your creatures.
> I wish no more than this, O Lord.
> Into your hands I commend my soul;
> I offer it to you
> with all the love of my heart,
> for I love you, Lord,
> and so need to give myself,
> to surrender myself into your hands,

without reserve,
and with boundless confidence,
for you are my Father.   Amen.
Charles de Foucald (1858–1916)

7 The door into the world

But you, dear friends, *build* yourselves up in your most
holy faith and *pray* in the Holy Spirit. *Keep* yourselves in
God's love as you *wait* for the mercy of our Lord Jesus
Christ to bring you to eternal life.

Jude 20f

Build us up, Lord Jesus, in our most holy faith;
Pray in us, Holy Spirit, with sounds too deep for words;
Keep us always in your love, Father, that we may
Wait for your mercy, one God in Trinity, to bring us to
    eternal life.   Amen.

To him who is able to keep *us* from falling and to present
us before his glorious presence without fault and with
great joy – to the only God our Saviour be glory, majesty,
power and authority, through Jesus Christ our Lord,
before all ages, now and for evermore!   Amen.

Jude 24f

DAY 26

THE CHRISTIAN LISTENER

1 *The entrance to the house of God's glory*

Speak, Lord, for your servant is listening.

1 Samuel 3: 9

Coming to terms with silence is a necessary element in self-knowledge and in prayer. Pascal claimed that 'most of man's troubles come from his not being able to sit quietly in his room.'

The purpose of silence is to allow the heart to be still and to listen to God. To build up inner resources of silence and stillness is one of the central tasks of training in prayer. In a culture which has almost outlawed silence, it is a matter of urgency that Christians create oases, centres in which inner silence can be cultivated.

Kenneth Leech, Soul Friend, Sheldon Press 1977

Help us, O Lord, to find time to be quiet. Sometimes our ears get so bombarded with noise that we don't hear anything. Help us to learn to listen. If we begin to hear tiny sounds – quiet breathing, the murmur of bees, the rustling of leaves; then we may begin to hear what people are trying to say to us. And what YOU may be saying. Let us remember the deaf in their loneliness and isolation. But we may be isolated by noise. Open our ears, Lord. Amen.

Sue Jeffreys

Father, as you revealed yourself to Samuel through
    your word,
  So continue to assure us of your presence;

And through our prayerful listening to your word,
    our silence and our stillness,
Guide us and give us discernment in all things for
        your glory.
Speak, Lord, your servant is listening – today.
Amen.

2 *The therapy room*

I have just hung up, why did he telephone?
I don't know . . . Oh! I get it . . .
I talked a lot and listened very little.

Forgive me, Lord, it was a monologue and not a
    dialogue.
I explained my idea and did not get his;
Since I didn't listen, I learned nothing,
Since I didn't listen, I didn't help,
Since I didn't listen, we didn't communicate.

Forgive me, Lord, for we were connected,
And now we are cut off.

                    Michel Quoist, *Prayers of Life*

O Lord Jesus, give us hearts that listen.
Hearts that listen to Thee in silence and love.
Hearts that listen to those we meet,
                    to those in trouble,
in the silence of true compassion,
Thy compassion and understanding.
Help us to remember that there is a time for silence
    and a time for speaking
and give us the wisdom to know when to speak
    and when to hold our peace.
Forgive us all the times we have failed to listen
and so missed the chance to help,
leaving our friend uncomforted.
    Silence us, O Lord, for Thy Name's
        sake.   Amen.

                    Elizabeth Basset, *Love is My Meaning*,
                    Darton, Longman & Todd 1973

3 The library

Counselling is understood by many to be a way in which one person listens to another and guides him or her to better self-understanding and greater emotional independence. But it is also possible to experience the relationship between counsellor and the person he or she is counselling as a way of entering together into the loving silence of God and waiting there for the healing Word. The Holy Spirit is called the divine Counsellor. He is actively present in the lives of those who come together to discern God's will. This is why human counsellors should see as their primary task the work of helping others to become aware of the movements of the divine Counsellor and encouraging them to follow these movements without fear. In this perspective, pastoral counselling is the attempt to lead fearful people into the silence of God, and to help them feel at home there, trusting that they will slowly discover the healing presence of the Spirit.

This suggests that the human counsellor needs to be very sensitive to the words of Scripture as words emerging from God's silence and directed to specific people in specific circumstances. When a word from Scripture is spoken by a counsellor at that particular moment when a person is able to hear it, it can indeed shatter huge walls of fear and open up unexpected perspectives. Such a word then brings with it the divine silence from which it came and to which it returns.

Henri J. M. Nouwen, *The Way of the Heart*,
Darton, Longman & Todd 1981

4 The music room

Rise and hear! The Lord is speaking,
as the gospel words unfold;
man, in all his agelong seeking,
finds no firmer truth to hold.

Word of goodness, truth, and beauty,
heard by simple folk and wise,
word of freedom, word of duty,
word of life beyond our eyes.

Word of God's forgiveness granted
  to the wild or guilty soul,
word of love that works undaunted,
  changes, heals, and makes us whole.

Speak to us, O Lord, believing,
  as we hear, the sower sows;
may our hearts, your word receiving,
  be the good ground where it grows.
                 H. C. A Gaunt (1902–   ) HFT 176

5 *The quiet room*

The Sovereign Lord has given me an instructed
    tongue,
  to know the word that sustains the weary.
He wakens me morning by morning,
  wakens my ear to listen like one being taught.
The Sovereign Lord has opened my ears,
  and I have not been rebellious; I have not drawn
    back.

                                    Isaiah 50: 4, 5

Speak, Lord, for your servant is listening.
                                    1 Samuel 3: 9

*   *   *   *

It is not the listener's job to go round ripping off people's
masks (however clearly he thinks he can see them).
No-one puts on a mask without first of all needing to do
so. At some point earlier on in life he apparently felt he
could not cope without a defence, so on went the mask
and he discovered that life was more comfortable living
behind it. But, as Christians, we are told to walk in the
light and grow in the truth, and there come times for all of
us when we have the opportunity of removing the mask
and living more truthfully (and perhaps more vulner-
ably). This might happen because we see an openness
and honesty in someone else, and we wish we could be
like them. And the challenge here for the listener is to
be the kind of person who makes it easy for people to
come out from behind their masks and defences, and to
share their humanity with the listener, feeling that it is
acceptable to do so. Quite a challenging business!

The listener's job then, is not to condemn or point the finger, or expose in a threatening way, but to invite openness by demonstrating it in himself. Then, when a person is ready to raise the blinds and share the reality of himself, this can lead to growth and change.

Anne Long

* * * *

Sovereign Lord, waken me morning by morning
    that I may listen as one being taught;
Teach me such an openness to you and your glory
    that I may help others to be open to you also;

Give me an instructed tongue
    that I may listen for your word which will
      sustain the weary;
So may we all grow more into your likeness
    and never draw back from following you,
      our Sovereign Lord.   Amen.

Speak, Lord, for your servant is listening . . .

6 The living room

Jesus said (to his disciples,) 'Let the children come to me, and do not hinder them, for the kingdom of heaven belongs to such as these.'

Matthew 19: 14

Lord, may I listen to this word of yours and take it
    to my heart.
Too often it is children for whom we have so little
    time, and so they go unheard, with no-one to
    listen to them.
Today I pray for the children of this land and every
    land; especially for those who are unhappy,
    unwanted or unloved, hungry or cold,
    frightened or ill.
For those who live in homes made unhappy by
    quarrels.
For the children of divorced parents, children who
    do not know to whom to give their allegiance or
    from whom to seek love.
Give them, O Lord, some person who will listen to

them today; may they find comfort and some
   means by which they are loved and honoured,
   their conflicts solved and their inner security
   maintained.
Teach us to remember that the kingdom of heaven
   is only open to the childlike;
   that children are the only assets of the future,
   the only means by which our ideals can survive
   and our dreams come true.
Let us never despise one of these little ones, and
   may we never pass one by who needs to be
   listened to, for their angels behold the face of our
   Father in heaven.   Amen.

> Adapted from a prayer by Leslie Weatherhead,
> *A Private House of Prayer*, 15, 6

7 *The door into the world*

A bright cloud enveloped them, and a voice from the
cloud said, 'This is my Son, whom I love; with him I am
well pleased. Listen to him!'

> Matthew 17: 5

Father, you have told us to listen to your Son; give
   us ears to hear his lightest whisper.
The daily work and the rush of life around us, and
   the clamour of our own fears and self-concern,
   make such a noise that it is difficult to be quiet
   before you.
And so we lose the sound of his voice.
Teach us how to be more still.
Teach us how to shut our doors around us to all
   other thoughts, and to make a deep silence in
   our hearts.
Then when he speaks to us, we shall be strong to
   hear, strong to do, strong to follow his call
   utterly.
We ask it in his name, Jesus Christ our
   Lord.   Amen.

> Adapted from a prayer in *Prayers of Health and Healing*

May God give us grace to listen to him and to his creation,
now and all our days.   Amen.

DAY 27

THE HEALING LOVE
OF CHRIST

1 *The entrance to the house of God's glory*

We know that we have passed from death to life, because
we love our brothers. Anyone who does not love remains
in death.
This is how we know what love is: Jesus Christ laid down
his life for us. And we ought to lay down our lives for our
brothers.
Let us not love with words or tongue but with actions and
in truth.
And this is his command: to believe in the name of
his Son, Jesus Christ, and to love one another as he
commanded us.

1 John 3: 14, 16, 18, 23

> I did not think, I did not strive,
> The deep peace burnt my me alive;
> The bolted door had broken in,
> I knew that I had done with sin.
> I knew that Christ had given me birth
> To brother all the souls on earth,
> And every bird and every beast
> Should share the crumbs broke at the feast.
>
> John Masefield, *The Everlasting Mercy*

May the same mind be in us which was in Christ Jesus;
that having his love, his humility, and his obedience
always in remembrance, we may consecrate ourselves to
the service of others, in his name and for his sake.
Amen.

Christ our Saviour, when you beheld the people you were moved with compassion towards them and healed the sick, fed the hungry, and raised the fallen. Pour out upon your Church the same spirit of love. Go forth with all who minister in your name to relieve suffering; and grant that by their service the hearts of men may be drawn to you.   Amen.

New Every Morning, p 112, BBC 1974

2 *The therapy room*

Great and glorious God, my Lord Jesus Christ!
   Fill me with light.
   Disperse the darkness of my soul.
   Give me true faith,
      firm hope,
      and perfect love.
Enable me, O Lord, to know you so well
   that in all things I may live by
      your healing light and love,
   and in accordance with your holy will.
   Amen.

After St Francis of Assisi (1182–1226)
(Another version is to be found in *Prayers for Today*
edited Norman Goodacre, Mowbrays 1972)

3 *The library*

As soon as they left the synagogue, they went with James and John to the home of Simon and Andrew. Simon's mother-in-law was in bed with a fever, and they told Jesus about her. So he went to her, took her hand and helped her up. The fever left her and she began to wait on them.

That evening after sunset the people brought to Jesus all the sick and demon-possessed. The whole town gathered at the door, and Jesus healed many who had various diseases.

A man with leprosy came to him and begged him on his knees, 'If you are willing, you can make me clean.'

Filled with compassion, Jesus reached out his hand and touched the man. 'I am willing,' he said. 'Be clean!' Immediately the leprosy left him and he was cured.

Jesus sent him away at once with a strong warning. 'See that you don't tell this to anyone. But go, show yourself to the priest and offer the sacrifices that Moses commanded for your cleansing, as a testimony to them.' Instead he went out and began to talk freely, spreading the news. As a result, Jesus could no longer enter a town openly but stayed outside in lonely places. Yet the people still came to him from everywhere.

Mark 1: 29–34a, 40–45

Jesus's healing work was totally consonant with his person and his teaching. His healings found their origin in the essential nature of God and were a direct expression of his incarnation. He loved people – he was the human expression of the divine love of God for his creation, 'God so loved the world . . .' – and was utterly caring and compassionate. Compassion is the act of knowing and feeling suffering together. He suffered along with his people because he had to be tested in all points like them apart from sin. His healings flowed naturally from a nature that was essentially compassionate: they were not only the expression but the logical result of the incarnation. The recording of one after another especially in the Marcan groupings demonstrates how dedicated Jesus was to ministering to people with mental and physical diseases, so much so that in order that the work should continue, he commanded his disciples to do the same.

This healing and caring ministry is all of a piece with his teaching on caring and having compassion for one's neighbour. The prime example is of course the parable of the Good Samaritan which has caught the imagination down the centuries and has been the inspiration to millions as the expression of what lies at the heart of Christianity. Many have seen in the Samaritan the person of Christ himself, who *comes where we are* and ministers to our many wounds. This is the caring in depth that man needs and Christ came to give. It is an expression of God's limitless love, that he is putting the world to rights and cares desperately for his people. They have a right to sit in his Kingdom and Jesus's caring and compassion shown in his healing ministry is direct evidence that the Kingdom is breaking forth.

M. M., *The Christian Healing Ministry*, pp 58f

4 The music room

> Praise to the Holiest in the height,
>   And in the depth be praise,
> In all his words most wonderful,
>   Most sure in all his ways.
>
> O loving wisdom of our God!
>   When all was sin and shame,
> A second Adam to the fight
>   And to the rescue came.
>
> O wisest love! that flesh and blood
>   Which did in Adam fail,
> Should strive afresh against their foe,
>   Should strive and should prevail;
>
> O generous love! that he who smote
>   In Man for man the foe,
> The double agony in Man
>   For man should undergo;
>
> Praise to the Holiest in the height,
>   And in the depth be praise,
> In all his words most wonderful,
>   Most sure in all his ways.
>   J. H. Newman (1801–90), EH 471

This famous hymn comes from Newman's poem *Gerontius*, which has lent its name to one of the hymn's most majestic tunes. The poem also inspired the music for one of the greatest of all English oratorios, Elgar's *The Dream of Gerontius*, first performed in 1900.

5 *The quiet room*

If I speak in the tongues of men and of angels, but have
not love, I am only a resounding gong or a clanging
cymbal. If I have the gift of prophecy and can fathom all
mysteries and all knowledge, and if I have a faith that can
move mountains, but have not love, I am nothing. If I
give all I possess to the poor and surrender my body to
the flames, but have not love, I gain nothing.

Love is patient, love is kind. It does not envy, it does
not boast, it is not proud. It is not rude, it is not self-
seeking, it is not easily angered, it keeps no record of
wrongs. Love does not delight in evil but rejoices with
the truth. It always protects, always trusts, always
hopes, always perseveres.

Love never fails. But where there are prophecies, they
will cease; where there are tongues, they will be stilled;
where there is knowledge, it will pass away. For we
know in part and we prophesy in part, but when perfection comes, the imperfect disappears. When I was a
child, I talked like a child, I thought like a child, I
reasoned like a child. When I became a man, I put
childish ways behind me. Now we see but a poor reflection; then we shall see face to face. Now I know in part;
then I shall know fully, even as I am fully known.

And now these three remain: faith, hope and love. But
the greatest of these is love.

1 Corinthians 13

Let us dwell on each phrase in the second paragraph:
Love is patient . . . Love is kind . . . and ask ourselves, Am
I? . . . Do I?

*   *   *   *

Let us realise that in our own life, in all our relationships
and dealings with others, the way of LOVE NEVER FAILS.

*   *   *   *

Lord Jesus, as I gaze at you on the cross, I wonder at so great
a redemption and the allness of your healing love.   Amen.

6 *The living room*

Lord Jesus Christ, you healed all who came to you in faith
and commissioned your Church not only to preach but to
heal: we bring to your healing love today our sick friends
. . . May your healing touch restore them to that perfect
health of spirit, mind and body, which is your will. We
ask this in your holy name of Jesus, our Healer and
Redeemer.   Amen.

Adapted from a prayer by H. C. Robins, one time
Dean of Salisbury

O God, you sent your Son to heal mankind in all its ills of
soul and mind and body: grant to your suffering servants
    his love to draw them closer to himself,
    his power to deliver them from all ills,
    and his joy and peace within their souls;
through the same Jesus Christ, whose healing love is
shed abroad in our hearts by the Holy Spirit, to your glory
heavenly Father, one God for all eternity.   Amen.

Adapted from a prayer by H. W. Bradfield, one time
Bishop of Bath and Wells

Both prayers are taken from *Prayers for Christian Healing*,
compiled by A. E. Campion, Mowbrays 1959.

7 *The door into the world*

The healing ministry is the logical result of the incarnation. God so loved the world that he gave his only
begotten Son; Jesus so loved that he healed. His healings
were the authentication of his mission and his person.
They flowed naturally from him because he was what he
was.

Morton Kelsey, *Healing and Christianity*, p 89, SCM Press 1973

Thank you, O God, for your love,
    and for all that you have done for me.
Help me to do more for you,
    and to live only and always for your glory;
for Jesus Christ's sake.   Amen.

Frank Colquhoun, NPP 557

To God the Father, who first loved us, and made
  us accepted
        in the Beloved;
to God the Son, who loved us, and washed us from
  our sins
        in his own blood;
to God the Holy Ghost, who sheds the love of God
  abroad
        in our hearts;
to the one true God be all love and all glory,
        for time and for eternity.   Amen.
      Thomas Ken, Bishop of Bath and Wells (1637–1711)

DAY 28

THE HEALING OF
THE NATIONS

1 *The entrance to the house of God's glory*

Then the angel showed me the river of the water of life, as
clear as crystal, flowing from the throne of God and of the
Lamb down the middle of the great street of the city. On
each side of the river stood the tree of life, bearing twelve
crops of fruit, yielding its fruit every month. And the
leaves of the tree are for *the healing of the nations*.

Revelation 22: 1, 2

The world is charged with the grandeur of God.
Gerard Manley Hopkins (1844–89)

Almighty and everliving God,
whose Son Jesus Christ healed the sick
and restored them to wholeness of life:
look with compassion on the anguish of the world,
and by your healing power
make whole both men and nations;
through our Lord and Saviour Jesus Christ,
who is alive and reigns with you and the Holy
    Spirit,
one God, now and for ever.   Amen.
                ASB, Collect for 8th Sunday before Easter

2 *The therapy room*

Father, as I pray today for the healing of the
    nations,

I come before you in penitence for the sins of
    my own nation:
For all the blood shed on our soil
– in the invasions during our early history,
    Lord, have mercy;
– in the civil wars we have waged among
    ourselves,
    Christ, have mercy;
– in the hurts we have inflicted on each other,
    Lord, have mercy;
For the blood we have shed on the soil of others
– in the days of Empire or greater wars,
    Holy and Blessed Trinity, have mercy.
Jesus, Saviour of humankind, who died for the sins
    of the whole world, forgive us:
heal us from the sins of the fathers being
    visited on the children;
heal us from the hatreds and resentments
    being carried on across generations;
heal us from the harm we continue to inflict on
    each other;
heal us, Christ our Healer.
Holy Spirit, bear your fruit of love and joy and
    peace among us, again in our time:
impart to us your holiness, that we may
    become a holy people;
lead us into all truth, that we may hear again
    your call to be a chosen generation;
give us life, that your grace may be manifested
    in the life of the nation.
Holy and Blessed Trinity, hear us, and when you
    hear, forgive;
for yours is the kingdom, the power and the
    glory, for ever and ever.   Amen.

3 *The library*

Prayers just for the peace of the world are not really what
we are being called to aim at. It's something much
deeper, much higher, infinitely more worthwhile. It's
praying for the coming of God's Kingdom *and for the*

coming of the Day of the Lord. Read the last two chapters of
the Bible to get a picture of it.

The kind of peace God wants for the earth is the kind of
peace that the Christian already knows, the peace that
does not originate in this world. It is Christ's peace. It is
that peace which is the fruit of the Spirit. To pray for the
peace of the world without being primarily mindful of
these greater things is simply praying that the symptoms
of the world's illness may be made easier to bear! What
we have to pray for is the *healing* of the world. And the
healing of the world begins when mankind breaks its
own heart into the agelong heartbreak of Christ and
accepts His will.

George Bennett, *Commissioned to Heal*, p 63,
Arthur James 1979

4 *The music room*

For the healing of the nations,
  Lord, we pray with one accord;
For a just and equal sharing
  of the things that earth affords.
To a life of love in action
  help us rise and pledge our word.

Lead us, Father, into freedom,
  from despair your world release;
That, redeemed from war and hatred,
  men may come and go in peace.
Show us how through care and goodness
  fear will die and hope increase.

All that kills abundant living,
  let it from the earth be banned;
Pride of status, race or schooling,
  dogmas keeping man from man.
In our common quest for justice
  may we hallow life's brief span.

You, creator-God, have written
  your great name on all mankind;
For our growing in your likeness
  bring the life of Christ to mind;

That by our response and service
earth its destiny may find.
Fred Kaan (1929–   ), HFT 28

5 *The quiet room*

Then the angel showed me the river of the water of life, as
clear as crystal, flowing from the throne of God and of the
Lamb down the middle of the great street of the city. On
each side of the river stood the tree of life, bearing twelve
crops of fruit, yielding its fruit every month. And the
leaves of the tree are for the healing of the nations. No longer
will there be any curse. The throne of God and of the
Lamb will be in the city, and his servants will serve him.
They will see his face, and his name will be on their
foreheads. There will be no more night. They will not
need the light of a lamp or the light of the sun, for the
Lord God will give them light. And they will reign for
ever and ever.

Revelation 22: 1–5

* * * *

In the chapel of King's College Hospital, London there is a
mosaic behind the altar of this wonderful scene from the
final chapter of our Bible. It centres the minds of the
worshippers on the Christ who came to heal all peoples and
nations.

There is also a tapestry depicting the tree whose leaves
are for the healing of the nations in the Corrymeela Community in Northern Ireland, a community dedicated to
reconciliation, healing and peace. Let us make a mental
picture of this scene as we read it and centre our thoughts
on the Christ who *is healing* the nations.

* * * *

Let us ponder what the healing of the nations might
actually bring:

Not only peace but joy in all creation and the perfect love
that casts out fear.
Truth and justice, and a complete care for all in society.
A true healing of all relationships.
Unity, a true oneness in Christ, for the Church.

Harmony for the animal kingdom.
The nearer approach of *God's Kingdom.*
God, and God alone.

* * * *

May the kingdoms of this world become the Kingdom of
our God and of his Christ.   Amen.
Thy Kingdom come.   Amen.

* * * *

6 *The living room*

Lord Jesus Christ,
who brought healing to the multitudes
and bestowed the Easter gift of peace on your
    disciples;
we look out on a world in need of your healing gift,
    a world divided between the haves and the
        have-nots,
        disintegrated by class and colour and creed,
        destroyed by wars and rumours of wars,
        dissipated by misuse and abuse of the good
            things you give us richly to enjoy,
        dis-eased by sicknesses we have brought
            upon ourselves.
Come and reign in the hearts of men and women
    everywhere, bringing your healing to the
    kingdoms of this world.
Give to us a vision of the peace of God that passes
    all understanding,
    a foretaste of the healing of heaven;
so that we may truly be your peace-making sons
    and daughters,
    reconciling the divided,
    unifying the disintegrated,
    ministering to the destitute and destroyed,
    raising up the dissipated,
    healing the dis-eased.
Then may your Kingdom of peace and justice,
    of serenity and well-being,
    of healing and true *shalom*
    enfold into its life the kingdoms of this world,

giving glory to the Father in the power of
the Holy Spirit.
          We ask it in your holy name.   Amen.

7 The door into the world

          Great and marvellous are your deeds,
               Lord God Almighty.
          Just and true are your ways,
               King of the ages.
          Who will not fear you, O Lord,
               and bring glory to your name?
          For you alone are holy.
          All nations will come
               and worship before you,
          for your righteous acts
               have been revealed.
                    Revelation 15: 3, 4

Give healing and peace in our time, O Lord:
     healing and reconciliation among the nations;
healing and harmony in our communities and our
          homes;
     healing and love in all our hearts;
for the sake of Jesus Christ, our Healer.   Amen.
               Adapted from Frank Colquhoun, NPP 176

The kingdom of the world has become the
               kingdom of our Lord
               and of his Christ,
and he will reign for ever and ever . . .
We give thanks to you, Lord God Almighty,
               who is and who was,
because you have taken your great power
               and have begun to reign.
                    Revelation 11: 15, 17

Blessing and honour, thanksgiving and praise,
               more than we can utter,
be unto thee, O most adorable Trinity,
               Father, Son, and Holy Ghost,
by all angels, all men, all creatures,
               for ever and ever.   Amen.
                    Bishop Thomas Ken (1637–1711)

DAY 29

THE KINGDOM OF GOD

1 *The entrance to the house of God's glory*

Seek first his kingdom and his righteousness, and all
these things will be given to you as well.

Matthew 6: 33

Through the incarnation of his Son, God initiated the task
of putting the world to rights. As we shall see, Jesus
encapsulated his vision of a healed creation in terms of
the Kingdom of God, his Father reigning in every part of
his creation. He 'earthed' this vision supremely in his
healing ministry, as he went about 'healing people who
had all kinds of disease and sickness' (Matthew 4: 23; 9: 35
etc.). He met people exactly where they were, at their
point of need. And he met every need, not just their
physical need, but their mental anguish or spiritual disability also. His healing was truly wholistic. He lifted
people out of the mess in which they found themselves,
sometimes through no fault of their own, and set them on
their way again, their journey to wholeness. He gave
them a new vision for life.

M. M., *Journey to Wholeness*, pp 7f

Grant us to look with your own eyes of compassion,
O merciful God, at the long travail of mankind:
> the wars, the hungry millions,
> the countless refugees,
> the natural disasters,
> the cruel and needless deaths,
> men's inhumanity to one another,

the heartbreak and hopelessness of many lives.
Hasten the coming of your kingdom,
when nations shall be at peace,
　free from fear and free from want,
　with no more pain or tears,
　in the assurance of your love
　and the security of your will,
shown to us in Jesus Christ our Lord.

George Appleton, NPP 167

2 *The therapy room*

O God, to whom we pray for the coming of your king-
dom: let this be no vain repetition on our part.
　　　　　　LORD HAVE MERCY
Let your kingdom come in us, that all our thoughts,
desires and acts may be brought into captivity to Christ.
　　　　　　CHRIST HAVE MERCY
Then take our lives, Lord God, and make them the agents
of your kingdom, that through us your will may be done
on earth as it is in heaven, to the glory of your name.
　　　　　　LORD HAVE MERCY

New Every Morning, p 72, adapted, BBC

Our Father,
who art in heaven,
hallowed be thy name.
Thy kingdom come,
thy will be done
on earth, as it is in heaven.
Give us this day our daily bread;
and forgive us our trespasses
as we forgive those who trespass against us;
and lead us not into temptation,
but deliver us from evil.
For thine is the kingdom, the power and the glory,
for ever and ever.　Amen.

3 The library

Jesus's life and teaching were based on a deep conviction about the Kingdom. It was his Father's purpose to reign in his creation and that meant in the hearts of all people, especially in the hearts of the poor and the outcast. This conviction undergirded all Jesus's healing work and his care for the underprivileged. If the Church would be true to its Lord today, it must be rooted theologically in the Kingdom and express its theology in a deep commitment to, and outgoing concern for, the sick, the refugees, the underprivileged, the prisoners, the outcast, the poor. This is the healing ministry committed to the Church, for which it is equipped with the healing power of its risen Lord. That healing power was always available to Jesus in his ministry because of his constant communion with his Father. A Church which is in continual communion with its Lord in the power of the Spirit will find that the reservoir of power to heal never runs dry. The Lord's presence to a Church alert, watchful, and obedient ensures the presence of that power to heal.

All this and more was part of his healing work and was a significant indication that the rule of God had begun and that the divine power would continue to manifest itself in signs following until the Kingdom is revealed in a healed creation. It is for this reason that he called his disciples and commissioned them to continue his work. That call and commission are being heard and answered with renewed conviction in the present century.

M. M., *The Christian Healing Ministry*, pp 60, 61

4 The music room

Rejoice! the Lord is King!
Your Lord and King adore;
Mortals, give thanks and sing,
And triumph evermore:
Lift up your heart, lift up your voice;
Rejoice, again I say, rejoice.

Jesus, the Saviour, reigns,
The God of truth and love;
When he had purged our stains,
He took his seat above:
Lift up your heart, lift up your voice;
Rejoice, again I say, rejoice.

His kingdom cannot fail;
He rules o'er earth and heaven;
The keys of death and hell
Are to our Jesus given:
Lift up your heart, lift up your voice;
Rejoice, again I say, rejoice.

He sits at God's right hand
Till all his foes submit,
And bow to his command,
And fall beneath his feet:
Lift up your heart, lift up your voice;
Rejoice, again I say, rejoice.
Charles Wesley (1707–1788), AMR 216

As we read the words, let us also 'hear' Handel's majestic tune 'Gopsal', lifting up our hearts and rejoicing that *Jesus, the Saviour, reigns* and *His kingdom cannot fail*.

5 *The quiet room*

Jesus viewed the Kingdom as a new era of blessing for the 'poor'. He invited 'those who labour and are heavy laden' to come to him. He used these terms in the prophetic sense of those who are oppressed and thrown completely on God's mercy. For him they are the hungry, those who weep, the sick, those who labour and bear burdens, the least and the simple, the lost and sinners. It is these who need health and salvation from the Physician of life, not those who are well. The old attitudes enshrined in a severe orthodoxy must change to a realization of the blessedness of those who know their need of God. There could be no view of the Kingdom for Jesus which did not include the poor.

Thus viewed, the Kingdom will be the source of health

for all people. The God who reigns is the infinitely gracious and loving God whose will and purpose for his creation is health and wholeness.

M. M., *The Christian Healing Ministry*, p 20

* * * *

At that very time Jesus cured many who had diseases, sicknesses and evil spirits, and gave sight to many who were blind. So he replied to the messengers, 'Go back and report to John what you have seen and heard:

> The blind receive sight,
> the lame walk,
> those who have leprosy are cured,
> the deaf hear,
> the dead are raised,
> and the good news is preached to the poor.
> Blessed is the man who does not fall away
>   on account of me.'

Luke 7: 21–23

* * * *

What can I/my church/my praying group DO to ensure the 'poor' are hearing the good news of the Kingdom of God?

* * * *

THY KINGDOM COME.   Amen.

6 *The living room*

> It's a long way off but inside it
> There are quite different things going on:
> Festivals at which the poor man
> Is King, and the consumptive is
> Healed, mirrors in which the blind look
> At themselves and love looks at them
> Back; and industry is for mending
> The bent bones and the minds fractured
> by life. It's a long way off, but to get
> There takes no time, and admission

Is free, if you will purge yourself
of desire, and present yourself with
Your need only, and the simple offering
of your faith, green as a leaf.

R. S. Thomas, The Kingdom

Let us visualise this eternal festival of the Kingdom, where
'there are quite different things going on.'
In this context we see in the presence of the King Himself –
the poor
the sick
the blind
the crippled
the mentally sick
as *all part of His healed creation.*

*   *   *   *

Let us ask that we may gain admission ourselves to this
festival for it is free.
Let us ask for the grace – to purge our desires
– only to bring before him our
needs and the simple offering of
our faith, in all its tenderness of
new life.

*   *   *   *

Lord, heal your creation so that the festival of your Kingdom may begin on earth, as it is in heaven:
Lord, you have shown me it needs to begin in me. Thank
you.
Maranatha: even so come, Lord Jesus.   Amen.

7 *The door into the world*

The kingdom of the world has become the kingdom of
our Lord and of his Christ, and he will reign for ever and
ever.

Revelation 11: 15

The kingdom of God is not a matter of talk but of power.

1 Corinthians 4: 20

The Kingdom of God is not a territorial or static but a dynamic symbol. It refers to God reigning, God actively ruling in his royal power, God visiting and redeeming his people. It means that God is setting the world to rights, saving men from sin, sickness, and evil and establishing a new order of things.

M. M., *The Christian Healing Ministry*, p 18

Almighty God, we long for the time when your kingdom shall come on earth: when men and nations shall acknowledge your sovereignty, seek your glory, and serve your good and righteous will.

Help us not only to pray but also to work for that new day; and enable us by your grace to promote the cause of justice and peace, truth and freedom, both in our own society and in the life of the world; for the honour of Christ, our Saviour and our Lord. Amen.

Frank Colquhoun, CPP 307

For thine is the Kingdom, the power and the glory, for ever and ever. Amen.

DAY 30

THE WILL OF GOD

1 *The entrance to the house of God's glory*

Jesus went out as usual to the Mount of Olives, and his
disciples followed him. On reaching the place, he said to
them, 'Pray that you will not fall into temptation.' He
withdrew about a stone's throw beyond them, knelt
down and prayed, 'Father, if you are willing, take this
cup from me; yet *not my will, but yours be done.*' An angel
from heaven appeared to him and strengthened him.
And being in anguish, he prayed more earnestly, and his
sweat was like drops of blood falling to the ground.

When he rose from prayer and went back to the
disciples, he found them asleep, exhausted from sorrow.
'Why are you sleeping?' he asked them. 'Get up and pray
so that you will not fall into temptation.'

Luke 22: 39–46

Enlarge our souls with a divine charity, that we may hope
all things, endure all things; and become messengers of
Thy healing mercy to the grievances and infirmities of
men. In all things attune our hearts to the holiness and
harmony of Thy kingdom. And hasten the time when
Thy kingdom shall come, and *Thy will be done* on earth as
it is in heaven.   Amen.

James Martineau, HBCP 603

Our Father . . .

2 *The therapy room*

Have you no words? Ah, think again,
Words flow apace when you complain;

And fill your fellow-creature's ear
With the sad tale of all your care.

Were half the breath thus vainly spent,
To heaven in supplication sent;
Your cheerful song would oftener be
'Hear what the Lord has done for me'!
William Cowper (1731–1800)

If you will you can be cured. Deliver yourself to the physician, and he will cure the eyes of your soul and heart. Who is the physician? He is God, who heals and gives life through the Word and Wisdom.
St Theophilus of Antioch, from the first book addressed to
Autolycus, 2, 7

Grant us such grace that we may work Thy will,
And speak Thy words, and walk before Thy face,
Profound and calm like waters deep and still;
Grant us such grace.   Amen.
Christina Rossetti (1830–94), HBCP 199

3 The library

The will of God is the presence, the reality and the virtue of all things, adjusting them to souls. Without God's direction all is void, emptiness, vanity, words, superficiality, death. The will of God is the salvation, sanity and life of body and soul whatever else it may bring to either of them. Whether it be vexation and trouble for the mind, or sickness and death for the body, nevertheless that divine will remains all in all. Bread without the divine will is poison, with it true sustenance. Without the divine will reading only blinds and perplexes, with it it enlightens. The divine will is the wholeness, the good and the true in all things. Like God, the universal Being, it is manifest in everything. It is not necessary to look to the benefits received by the mind and body to judge of their virtue. These are of no significance. It is the will of God that gives everything, whatever it may be, the power to form Jesus Christ in the centre of our being. This will knows no limits.
Jean-Pierre de Caussade, *Self-abandonment to Divine Providence*,
translated Kitty Muggeridge and published as *The Sacrament of
the Present Moment*, Collins Fount 1981

4 The music room

When God has all that he should have of thy heart, when renouncing the will, judgment, tempers and inclinations of the old man, thou art wholly given up to the obedience of the light and spirit of God within thee, to will only his holy will, to love only in his love, to be wise only in his wisdom, then it is that *everything thou doest is as a song of praise*, and the common business of *thy life is a conforming to God's will* on earth, as Angels do in heaven.

William Law, *The Spirit of Prayer*

Thy way, not mine, O Lord,
    However dark it be;
Lead me by thine own hand,
    Choose out the path for me.

The kingdom that I seek
    Is thine, so let the way
That leads to it be thine,
    Else I must surely stray.

Not mine, not mine, the choice
    In things or great or small;
Be thou my Guide, my Strength,
    My Wisdom, and my All.

H. Bonar (1808–1889), EH 505

5 The quiet room

Let us, then, labour for an inward silence –
An inward stillness and an inward healing;
That perfect silence where the lips and heart
Are still, and we no longer entertain
Our own imperfect thoughts and vain opinions,
But God alone speaks in us, and we wait
In singleness of heart, *that we may know*
His will, and in the silence of our spirits,
That we may do His will, and do that only.

Henry Wadsworth Longfellow (1807–82)

God alone speaks in us . . .
We wait in singleness of heart . . .
That we may know his will . . .

And in the silence of our spirits . . .
THAT WE MAY DO HIS WILL AND DO THAT ONLY.

*   *   *   *

> Renew my will from day to day,
> Blend it with Thine, and take away
> All that now makes it hard to say,
> Thy will be done.
>
> Charlotte Elliott, HBCP 175

*   *   *   *

O thou who art heroic love, keep alive in our hearts that adventurous spirit which makes men scorn the way of safety, so that thy will be done. For so only, O Lord, shall we be worthy of those courageous souls who in every age have ventured all in obedience to thy call, and for whom the trumpets have sounded on the other side; through Jesus Christ our Lord.   Amen.

J. H. Oldham, HBCP 184

6 The living room

For the healing of political life:

Grant and continue unto us, O Lord, a succession of legislators and rulers who have been taught the wisdom of the kingdom of Christ. Endow all members of Parliament with a right understanding, a pure purpose, and sound speech; enable them to rise above all self-seeking and party zeal into the larger sentiments of public good and human brotherhood. Purge our political life of every evil; subdue in the nation all unhallowed thirst for conquest or vainglory. Inspire us with calmness and self-restraint and the endeavour to get thy will done everywhere upon earth; through Jesus Christ our Lord.   Amen.

John Hunter (1845–1917), HBCP 936

For the healing of personal sickness:

Lord, bless all means that are used for my recovery, and restore me to my health in thy good time; but if otherwise thou hast appointed for me, thy blessed will be done. O draw me away from an affection for things below, and fill me with an ardent desire for heaven.

Lord, fit me for thyself, and then call me to those

joys unspeakable and full of glory, when thou pleas-
est, and that for the sake of thy only Son, Jesus, my
Saviour.   Amen.
> Thomas Ken, Bishop of Bath and Wells (1637–1711),
> HBCP 805

Teach us, good Lord, to serve you as you deserve;
>   to give and not to count the cost;
>   to fight and not to heed the wounds;
>   to toil and not to seek for rest;
>   to labour and not to ask for any reward,
>   save that of knowing that we do your will;
>   through Jesus Christ our Lord.   Amen.
> Ignatius de Loyola (1491–1556), HBCP 888

7 The door into the world

When we speak with God, our power of addressing Him,
of holding communion with Him, and listening to His
still small Voice, depends upon our will being one and
the same with His.
> Florence Nightingale (1820–1910)

Set before our minds and hearts, O heavenly Father, the
example of our Lord Jesus Christ, who, when he was
upon earth, found his refreshment in doing the will of
him that sent him, and in finishing his work. When many
are coming and going, and there is little leisure, give us
grace to remember him who knew neither impatience of
spirit nor confusion of work, but in the midst of all his
labours held communion with thee, and even upon earth
was still in heaven; where now he reigns with thee and
the Holy Spirit, world without end.   Amen.
> Dean Vaughan in Journey for a Soul by George Appleton,
> p 164, Collins Fontana 1974

The God of peace, who brought again from the dead our
Lord Jesus, that great shepherd of the sheep, through the
blood of the eternal covenant, make us perfect in every
good work to do his will, working in us that which is
well-pleasing in his sight; and may the blessing of God
almighty, the Father, the Son, and the Holy Spirit, be
upon us, and remain with us always.   Amen.
> Blessing for Easter, ASB

DAY 31

WHOLENESS

1 *The entrance to the house of God's glory*

Holy, holy, holy
is the Lord God Almighty,
who was, and is, and is to come.

Revelation 4: 8

Wholeness depends on being under the influence of the Holy Spirit.

O Spirit of God,
penetrate into the depths of our spirits,
into the storehouse of memories,
remembered and forgotten,
into the depths of being,
the very springs of personality,
and cleanse and forgive,
making us whole and holy,
that we may be thine
and live in the new being
of Christ our Lord. Amen.

George Appleton, *One Man's Prayers*,
p 14, SPCK 1967

2 *The therapy room*

O God, our Father, to whom the issues of life and death belong, preserve us from all ills.

Preserve us in health of body,
   that we may be able to earn a living for ourselves
   and for those whom we love.
Preserve us in soundness of mind,
   that all our judgments and decisions may be
   sane and wise.
Preserve us in purity of life,
   that we may conquer all temptation and ever do
   the right,
   that we may walk through the world and yet
   keep our garments unspotted from the world.

And if illness, misfortune, sorrow come to us, preserve us in courage, in endurance, and in serenity of faith, that, in all the changes and the chances of life, we may still face life with steady eyes, because we face life with you.
   This we ask for your love's sake.   Amen.
William Barclay, *Prayers for the Christian Year*, SCM Press 1964

3 *The library*

The reality of the spiritual and the primacy of the personal are intimately bound up with the Christian doctrine of the wholeness of personality. Today the growing understanding of the relation of mind and spirit to the body and to bodily ill-health, makes it easier to grasp the fact of the essential unity of man's nature; to realize that that unity implies a vital relationship between the healing of body, soul, and spirit. It is a fact of experience that just as skilled and compassionate care for man's physical needs often has spiritual effects, so also a wise and understanding ministry to man's spiritual needs may have direct physical effects. Harmony of the whole nature is the necessary condition for full health.

This truth is intuitively recognized by those for whom religion and medicine still retain their close relation. A deputation from one of the clinics attached to the Oji River Settlement (Nigeria) for the treatment of sufferers from leprosy came begging for more adequate Christian teaching. 'We want the Word of God before treatment,' they said. 'It is not well having the body strong if the heart inside is sick.'

Wholeness: how deep is the hunger for it, for God has made man for unity and is ever seeking to restore the divine image. His redemptive purpose is concerned with the whole of man's need and nature; with the renewing and fulfilling of his entire personality. As an instrument of that purpose the healing arm of the Church has a further essential contribution to make in the modern world through its witness to the fundamental unity of human personality, and the power of the Christian Gospel to meet the trinity of man's need.

Phyllis L. Garlick, *Man's Search For Health*, p 273,
The Highway Press 1952

4 *The music room*

A hymn for the wholeness of the healing
professions and for those to whom they minister.

O God, whose will is life and good
    for all of mortal breath,
Unite in bonds of brotherhood
    all those who fight with death.

Make strong their hands and hearts and wills
    to drive disease afar,
To battle with the body's ills,
    and wage thy holy war.

Where'er they heal the sick and blind,
    Christ's love may they proclaim;
Make known the good Physician's mind,
    and prove the Saviour's name.

Before them set thy holy will,
    that they, with heart and soul,
To thee may consecrate their skill,
    and make the sufferer whole.

H. D. Rawnsley (1851–1920), HFT 75

5 *The quiet room*

Secular society has not managed to solve the really deep problems. We still fear and wonder about death; we dread suffering. The consumer society – the society in which we are offered every kind of material good and prosperity – has not satisfied the deepest longings of the human heart or given the joy and contentment for which every heart craves. Jung in his book *Modern Man in Search of a Soul* wrote:

'. . . Among all my patients in the second half of life, there has not been one whose problem in the last resort was not that of finding a religious outlook on life. It is safe to say that every one of them fell ill because he had lost that which the living religions of every age have given their followers, and none of them has been really healed who did not regain his religious outlook.'

I have often thought about that, and it has led me to reflect that what is true for the individual is surely true also for the individual in his or her relationship with others, therefore in society itself. The patient may have much wrong with him, but he can be cured. There are always signs of hope, always good things to note. Indeed, whatever the signs to the contrary, there remains in each one of us at least a spark of religion to be ignited into something brighter and warmer. The promise of a healing process is there.

How do we detect this spark within us? I imagine that it is different for each person, which would not be surprising since every person is unique. I think it has something to do with a longing deep down within us. We long to know and possess the good, or the good that we see in a great number of persons and objects which fall within our experience. In the end we discover that the pursuit of truth and goodness leads us to long for truth and goodness in their absolute form. This absolute truth and this absolute goodness we call God.

There are threats to life and the quality of life. Individuals and society cannot be fundamentally healed without a radical transformation. Religion is essential to this process. Personal renewal and renewal of society follow the same pattern. A return to God is a precondition for a return to health.

Basil Hume, To Be a Pilgrim, St Paul Publications

* * * *

Let us pray that this spark may be ignited deep within us that will give us that longing for the wholly good – for God himself:

> Lord of all power and might,
> who art the author and giver of all good things;
> Graft in our hearts the love of thy Name,
> increase in us true religion,
> nourish us with all goodness,
> and of thy great mercy keep us in the same;
> through Jesus Christ our Lord.   Amen.

Collect for the Seventh Sunday after Trinity, BCP

6 *The living room*

The methods Jesus used with such effect upon the sick were actions which appear to have done two things. They awakened the spirit that lay deep within these people, waiting to be touched. And at the same time his actions, words, and attitudes brought contact with the Spirit of God, the creative force of reality, which sets men's minds and bodies aright and recreates them. Deep spoke to deep, through sacramental action. The nature of his healing, its essential method, was sacramental, religious. *Through him the power of God broke through into the lives of men, and they were made whole.* There is little more that one can say.

Morton T. Kelsey, Healing and Christianity, SCM Press 1973

As we recall at leisure the times when the power of God broke through into the lives of men and women, both during the days of Jesus' ministry on earth as well as the present time as he ministers to people through his Body, the Church, *to make them whole*, let us quietly ask him that his power will break through into
  – my life;

– the lives of those I shall meet this day;
– each one for whom I feel a burden of concern.

*   *   *   *

A prayer for those in suffering:

Heavenly Father, we commend to your love
and care those who suffer in body, mind or spirit,
and especially those known to us
whom we hold up to you in silence now . . .
In your goodness and mercy grant them
health of body,
soundness of mind,
and peace of heart,
that in wholeness of being they may glorify your name,
through Jesus Christ our Lord.   Amen.
                                    Frank Colquhoun, NPP 287

7 The door into the world

I will extol the Lord at all times;
his praise will always be on my lips.
My soul will boast in the Lord;
let the afflicted hear and rejoice.
Glorify the Lord with me;
let us exalt his name together.
I sought the Lord, and he answered me;
he delivered me from all my fears.
Those who look to him are radiant;
their faces are never covered with shame.
Taste and see that the Lord is good;
blessed is the man who takes refuge in him.
                                    Psalm 34: 1–5, 8

There is a new awareness of the need for inter-
disciplinary research and reflection, based on a new
holistic vision which requires the co-operation of the
various competences. As the insight dawns in some
circles of scientists and doctors that health and sickness
cannot really be understood if the dimensions of salvation and wholeness are ignored, so too, theologians
are beginning to realize that they will inevitably fall short

of a holistic vision of man unless all the insights of the various disciplines that go to the study of the human person and the condition of human life are integrated.

Bernard Häring, *Healing and Revealing*, p 8, St Paul 1984

Almighty and everliving God,
whose Son Jesus Christ healed the sick
and restored them to wholeness of life:
look with compassion on the anguish of the world,
and by your healing power
make whole both men and nations;
through our Lord and Saviour Jesus Christ,
who is alive and reigns with you and the Holy
   Spirit,
one God, now and for ever.   Amen.

Collect for 8th Sunday before Easter, ASB

The grace of the Lord Jesus be with God's people.

Amen.

ROOMS
FOR
THE
CHURCH'S
SEASONS

ADVENT

1 *The entrance to the house of God's glory*

O Wisdom, who camest out of the mouth of the Most High, and reachest from one end to another, mightily and sweetly ordering all things: Come and teach us the way of prudence.

O Adonai, and leader of the house of Israel, who didst appear in the bush to Moses in a flame of fire, and gavest him the law on Sinai: Come and redeem us with an outstretched arm.

O Root of Jesse, who standest for an ensign of the people, at whom kings shall shut their mouths, unto whom shall the Gentiles seek: Come and deliver us, and tarry not.

O Key of David, and sceptre of the house of Israel, who openest and no man shutteth, and shuttest and no man openeth: Come, and bring the prisoners out of the prison-house, them that sit in darkness and the shadow of death.

O Day-spring, brightness of the light everlasting, and sun of righteousness: Come and enlighten them that sit in darkness and the shadow of death.

O King of nations, and their desire; the cornerstone who makest both one: Come and save mankind, whom thou hast formed of clay.

O Emmanuel, our King and lawgiver, the desire of all nations and their salvation: Come and save us, O Lord our God.

O Virgin of virgins, how shall this be? for neither before thee was any seen like thee, nor shall there be after.

Daughters of Jerusalem, why do you marvel at me? The thing which you behold is a divine mystery.

The Greater Antiphons (Western Rite), used at Vespers or Evensong before and after the Magnificat, from December 16th to 23rd inclusive. They could be used on their appropriate day as a sentence for meditation, or at other times during the Advent season.

O Lord our God, make us watchful and keep us faithful as we await the coming of your Son our Lord; that when he shall appear he may find us not sleeping in sin but active in his service and joyful in his praise, for the glory of your holy name.   Amen.

Adapted from a Gelasian collect, CPP 4

2 *The therapy room*

Creator of the starry height,
Thy people's everlasting Light,
Jesu, Redeemer of us all,
Hear thou thy servants when they call.

Thou, sorrowing at the helpless cry
Of all creation doomed to die,
Didst come to save our fallen race
By healing gifts of heavenly grace.

At thy great name, exalted now,
All knees in lowly homage bow;
All things in heaven and earth adore,
And own thee King for evermore.

To God the Father, God the Son,
And God the Spirit, Three in One,
Praise, honour, might and glory be
From age to age eternally.   Amen.

Seventh-Century Advent Office Hymn,
AMR 45

Let us praise him for the 'healing gifts of heavenly grace' by which our lives have been enriched.

Let us also examine ourselves concerning those parts of our life which still need his loving and redeeming power.

3 *The library*

An Old Testament reading – prophesying the Lord's coming

Comfort, comfort my people, says your God.
Speak tenderly to Jerusalem, and proclaim to her
that her hard service has been completed,
that her sin has been paid for,
that she has received from the Lord's hand
    double for all her sins.
A voice of one calling:
'In the desert prepare the way for the Lord;
make straight in the wilderness a highway for our
    God.
Every valley shall be raised up,
    every mountain and hill made low;
the rough ground shall become level,
    the rugged places a plain.
And the glory of the Lord will be revealed
    and all mankind together will see it.
For the mouth of the Lord has spoken.'

                          Isaiah 40: 1- 5

A New Testament reading – rousing us to await our salvation/healing

And do this (loving your neighbour), understanding the
present time. The hour has come for you to wake up from
your slumber, because our salvation is nearer now than
when we first believed. The night is nearly over; the day
is almost here. So let us put aside the deeds of darkness
and put on the armour of light. Let us behave decently, as
in the daytime, not in orgies and drunkenness, not in
sexual immorality and debauchery, not in dissension and
jealousy. Rather, clothe yourselves with the Lord Jesus
Christ, and do not think about how to gratify the desires
of the sinful nature.

                          Romans 13: 11–14

A Gospel reading – in which Jesus foretells his second coming

There will be signs in the sun, moon and stars. On the
earth, nations will be in anguish and perplexity at the

roaring and tossing of the sea. Men will faint from terror, apprehensive of what is coming on the world, for the heavenly bodies will be shaken. At that time they will see the Son of Man coming in a cloud with power and great glory. When these things begin to take place, stand up and lift up your heads, because your redemption is drawing near.

Luke 21: 25–28

4 *The music room*

The great Advent Chorale is *Wachet auf* or *Sleepers, wake.* J. S. Bach harmonised the stately melody and also wrote a chorale prelude on the theme.

We sing it to the sixteenth-century words of P. Nicolai. Here are the first two verses, AMR 55

> Sleepers, wake! the watch-cry pealeth,
> While slumber deep each eyelid sealeth:
>   Awake, Jerusalem, awake!
> Midnight's solemn hour is tolling,
> And seraph-notes are onward rolling;
>   They call on us our part to take.
>   Come forth, ye virgins wise;
>   The Bridegroom comes, arise!
>   Alleluia!
>   Each lamp be bright
>   With ready light
> To grace the marriage feast to-night.

> Zion hears the voice that singeth,
> With sudden joy her glad heart springeth,
>   At once she wakes, she stands arrayed:
> Her Light is come, her Star ascending,
> Lo, girt with truth, with mercy blending,
>   Her Bridegroom there, so long delayed.
>   All hail! God's glorious Son,
>   All hail! our joy and crown,
>   Alleluia!
>   The joyful call
>   We answer all,
> And follow to the bridal hall.

5 *The quiet room*

Advent means 'coming'. In the Advent season we Christians come to the courts of waiting, seeking to be found watching when the Bridegroom comes. We pray – Maranatha: even so come, Lord Jesus. Let us be silent and await his coming.

* * * *

Prayer

> *Come*, thou long-expected Jesus,
>   Born to set thy people free;
> From our fears and sins release us;
>   Let us find our rest in thee.
>
> Israel's strength and consolation,
>   Hope of all the earth thou art;
> Dear Desire of every nation,
>   Joy of every longing heart.
>
> Born thy people to deliver;
>   Born a Child and yet a King;
> Born to reign in us for ever;
>   Now thy gracious kingdom bring.
>
> By thy own eternal Spirit,
>   Rule in all our hearts alone:
> By thy all-sufficient merit,
>   Raise us to thy glorious throne.
>   Charles Wesley (1707–1788), AMR 54

6 *The living room*

> Almighty God,
> give us grace to cast away the works of darkness
> and to put on the armour of light,
> now in the time of this mortal life,
> in which your Son Jesus Christ came to us in great
>   humility:
> so that on the last day,
> when he shall come again in his glorious majesty
>   to judge the living and the dead,
> we may rise to the life immortal;

through him who is alive and reigns with you and
the Holy Spirit,
one God, now and for ever.   Amen.

Advent Collect, BCP and ASB

Our heavenly Father, as once again we prepare for
Christmas, help us to find time in our busy lives for quiet
and thought and prayer; that we may reflect upon the
wonder of your love and allow the story of the Saviour's
birth to penetrate our hearts and minds . . .

Keep us mindful of the poverty-stricken peoples of the
world, the vast multitude who at this very time lack the
bare necessities of life . . .

Through the gifts we offer for their relief may we show
something of our gratitude for all that you have given us;
and may our gifts be acceptable through him who for our
sake became poor and was born in a stable, Jesus our
Saviour.   Amen.

Adapted from two prayers by Frank Colquhoun, CPP 18 and
NPP 75

7 *The door into the world*

Give us grace, O Lord, to live each day
    as if it were the day of your coming.
May we be urgent to prepare your way
    by fighting all evil,
    by preaching the gospel,
    by feeding the hungry,
    by releasing the oppressed,
    and by healing the sick.
So may we hasten the triumph of your kingdom,
    and bring glory to your name.   Amen.

John Kingsnorth, NPP 70

May Christ the Sun of Righteousness shine upon us
and scatter the darkness from before our path, and may
God, Father, Son and Holy Spirit bless us now and
always.   Amen.

ASB Advent blessing (adapted)

CHRISTMAS

1 *The entrance to the house of God's glory*

For to us a child is born,
  to us a son is given,
  and the government will be on his shoulders.
And he will be called
  Wonderful Counsellor, Mighty God,
  Everlasting Father, Prince of Peace.

Isaiah 9: 6

The Word became flesh and made his dwelling among
us. We have seen his glory, the glory of the One and Only
who came from the Father, full of grace and truth.

John 1: 14

Behold the great Creator makes
  Himself a house of clay,
A robe of Virgin flesh he takes
  Which he will wear for ay.

Hark, hark, the wise eternal Word,
  Like a weak infant cries!
In form of servant is the Lord,
  And God in cradle lies.

Glad shepherds ran to view this sight;
  A choir of Angels sings,
And eastern sages with delight
  Adore this King of kings.

Join then, all hearts that are not stone,
  And all our voices prove,
To celebrate this holy One
  The God of peace and love.

T. Pestel (1584–1659), EH 20

O come, let us adore him,
O come, let us adore him,
O come, let us adore him,
      Christ the Lord.   Amen.
      Eighteenth-century carol

2 *The therapy room*

Praise be to the Lord, the God of Israel,
   because he has come and has redeemed his
   people.
He has raised up a horn of salvation (healing) for
   us
   in the house of his servant David.
                        Luke 1: 68f

Hail the heaven-born Prince of peace!
Hail the Sun of Righteousness!
Light and life to all he brings,
Risen with healing in his wings;
Mild he lays his glory by,
Born that man no more may die,
Born to raise the sons of earth,
Born to give them second birth.
      Hark! the herald Angels sing
      Glory to the new-born King.
   Charles Wesley (1707–88) and others,
                  EH 24

A Christmas Day Prayer

Moonless darkness stands between
Past, O Past, no more be seen!
But the Bethlehem star may lead me
To the sight of Him who freed me
From the self that I have been.
Make me pure, Lord: Thou art holy;
Make me meek, Lord: Thou wert lowly;
Now beginning, and alway:
Now begin, on Christmas Day.
   Gerard Manley Hopkins (1844–1889)

3 *The library*

THE INCARNATION

According to St Irenaeus the object of the Incarnation was 'to join the end to the beginning, that is man to God', thus restoring to man what by the Fall he had lost. The Incarnation had a radical effect upon human nature, enabling man 'to share in the divinity of Christ, who humbled himself to share our humanity'.

In his divine and perfect life united with human nature Christ met the full force of evil, triumphing over it through obedience unto a real human death. His life, death and resurrection reveal the healing will of God, and through the operation of the Holy Spirit he brings man into vital contact with the life of God. He thus inaugurates a new phase of life for man, a life quickened by the Spirit through regeneration and incorporation into his Body, into which the believer normally enters by baptism. Through his Body the Spirit of God works the healing works of God.

The will of God to heal was seen throughout Christ's earthly mission, not only or primarily in the healing miracles, but in his teaching, calling men to care for the welfare of others, for example the parables of the Good Samaritan, Dives and Lazarus, the Prodigal Son, the Sheep and the Goats – to name only four. It is seen in his denunciation of the Pharisees, in fact throughout the whole Gospel story, culminating in his crucifixion for man's salvation.

This is in line with Old Testament teaching, especially according to the prophets. Love, justice and mercy are all characteristics of that out-going, self-sacrificing love which by its very nature heals; Christ heals because he is the embodiment of this love, and now as then brings blessings which benefit the whole man, working through his Body the Church, which has been described as the extension of the Incarnation. It is a fallacy to leave physical healing out of the picture although this has frequently been done in the past; it is the whole man who benefits. This was so well known and appreciated in the early days of Christianity that healing was a normal function. The

Acts of the Apostles and the other writings of the early Church are abundant evidence of this.

In the regenerate life, normally entered at baptism, man goes forward to his true destiny, and restlessness and disillusionment are replaced by a sense of purpose and meaning. As this life develops the healing fruits of the Spirit are seen. Love, joy, peace and so on, are as 'natural' to the regenerate life as the fruit is to its native tree. Life in line with the purpose of creation spells harmony, poise and health, not only for the individual but flowing out in healing to mankind.

Dame Raphael Frost, OSB, *Christ and Wholeness*, James Clarke

4 *The music room*

On Christmas night all Christians sing
To bear the news the angels bring:
News of great joy, news of great mirth,
News of our merciful King's birth.

When sin departs before thy grace,
Then life and health come in its place;
Angels and men with joy may sing,
All for to see the new-born King.

All out of darkness we have light,
Which made the angels sing this night;
'Glory to God and peace to men,
Now and for evermore. Amen'

This Traditional Sussex Carol has been arranged by Ralph Vaughan Williams (1872–1958) and is frequently heard in the Christmas Eve Carol Service broadcast annually from King's College, Cambridge.

5 *The quiet room*

READ Luke 2: 1–20

Visualise the scene at Bethlehem; feel yourself to be part of that scene; and, like Mary, ponder in your heart the beautiful words of the carol so that they become your own:

O little town of Bethlehem,
  How still we see thee lie!
Above thy deep and dreamless sleep
  The silent stars go by.
Yet in thy dark streets shineth
  The everlasting light;
The hopes and fears of all the years
  Are met in thee to-night.

O morning stars, together
  Proclaim the holy birth,
And praises sing to God the King,
  And peace to men on earth;
For Christ is born of Mary;
  And, gathered all above,
While mortals sleep, the angels keep
  Their watch of wondering love.

How silently, how silently,
  The wondrous gift is given!
So God imparts to human hearts
  The blessings of his heaven.
No ear may hear his coming;
  But in this world of sin,
Where meek souls will receive him, still
  The dear Christ enters in.

O holy Child of Bethlehem,
  Descend to us, we pray;
Cast out our sin, and enter in,
  Be born in us to-day.
We hear the Christmas Angels
  The great glad tidings tell:
O come to us, abide with us,
  Our Lord Emmanuel.
    Bishop Phillips Brooks (1835–93), EH 15

6 *The living room*

A Christmas Invocation

We bow before the cradle of the little Son of Peace and
pray that His spirit may fill our hearts; that the love that

sent Him may dominate our lives, that the faith which all His life sustained Him may be kindled in us. If we have come here proud or angry or aggressive; if we have come weary or depressed or sad; if we are cynical or cold or faithless, may we find that these mists of the soul disappear in the radiant sunshine of a royal love that stooped to a stable and yet is more enduring than the stars. O Saviour, Who didst come to men at Christmastime, we have come to adore Thee, Christ the Lord.   Amen.

A Christmas Day Prayer

We pray Thee, O Father, to bless all to whom even Christmas brings little of joy. For all who are racked with pain or overwhelmed in sorrow, for those who will spend the hours watching their loved ones suffer: for all who, far from home, are lonely and friendless and sad. We pray for all whose minds will fill with memories of other, brighter days when loved ones were with them who now have passed beyond these voices into the great silence. We pray for all who must spend the day in busy service for mankind on land and sea and in the air, and all who are too old to enjoy the Christmas fun. To them all may there come the Christmas message, and O God, bend us all more resolutely to the tasks of establishing that good-will among men that Thy peace may end all our tumult and confusion. Through Jesus Christ our Lord.   Amen.

Leslie Weatherhead, *A Private House of Prayer*

7 *The door into the world*

O God, whose love has been shown to us
   in the birth of Jesus our Saviour,
help us this Christmas to find time
   to let your love speak to us;
that we may respond to it
   in trust and adoration,
and open our hearts to receive
   your grace and pardon,
   your joy and peace,
through Jesus Christ our Lord.   Amen.

Adapted from NPP 80

May we now go forth in peace to love and serve the
     Lord,
  guided by the wisdom of the Wonderful
     Counsellor,
  defended by the strength of the Mighty God,
  enfolded in the love of the Everlasting Father,
  a sign of the peace of the Prince of Peace,
And may the blessing of God Almighty,
  the Father, the Son and the Holy Spirit
be upon us and all who are in our hearts,
  this Christmastide and always.   Amen.

* * * *

A New Year Dedication

All through this year, O Father,
  help us to know Christ better
  and to make him better known,
by yielding our wills to his lordship
  and our lives to the service of others;
for Jesus Christ's sake.   Amen.
Maurice Wood, CPP 46

* * * *

PASSIONTIDE

1 *The entrance to the house of God's glory*

May I never boast except in the cross of our Lord Jesus
Christ, through which the world has been crucified to
me, and I to the world.

Galatians 6: 14

The cross is a way of life; the way of love meeting all hate
with love, all evil with good, all negatives with positives.

Rufus Moseley

> O Lord Christ, Lamb of God, Lord of Lords,
> call us, who are called to be saints,
> along the way of thy cross:
> draw us, who would draw nearer our king,
> to the foot of thy cross:
> cleanse us, who are not worthy to approach,
> with the pardon of thy cross:
> instruct us, the ignorant and blind,
> in the school of thy cross:
> arm us, for the battles of holiness,
> by the might of thy cross:
> bring us in the fellowship of thy sufferings,
> to the victory of thy cross:
> and seal us in the kingdom of thy glory
> among the servants of thy cross,
> O crucified Lord;
> who with the Father and the Holy Ghost
> lives and reigns one God
> almighty, eternal,
> world without end.   Amen.

Eric Milner-White

2 *The therapy room*

> Soul of Christ, sanctify me.
> Body of Christ, save me.
> Blood of Christ, fill me.
> Water from the side of Christ, wash me.
> Passion of Christ, strengthen me.
> O good Jesus, hear me.
> Within your wounds hide me.
> Suffer me not to be separated from you.
> From the malicious enemy defend me.
> In the hour of my death call me.
> And bid me come unto you.
> That with your saints I may praise you.
> For ever and ever. Amen.
>
> Fourteenth-century prayer

3 *The library*

Now, I saw in my dream that the highway up which Christian was to go was fenced on either side with a wall that was called Salvation. Up this way, therefore, did burdened Christian run, but not without great difficulty, because of the load on his back.

He ran thus till he came to a place somewhat ascending; and upon that place stood a cross, and a little below, in the bottom, a sepulchre. So I saw in my dream that just as Christian came up with the cross, his burden loosed from off his shoulders, and fell from off his back, and began to tumble, and so continued to do till it came to the mouth of the sepulchre, where it fell in, and I saw it no more.

Then was Christian glad and lightsome, and said with a merry heart, 'He hath given me rest by his sorrow, and life by his death.' Then he stood still awhile to look and wonder; for it was very surprising to him that the sight of the cross should thus ease him of his burden. He looked, therefore, and looked again, even till the springs that were in his head sent the water down his cheeks.

Now, as he was looking and weeping, three Shining Ones came to him and saluted him with, 'Peace!'

So the first said to him, 'Your sins be forgiven you.' The second stripped him of his rags and clothed him with a change of raiment. The third also set a mark on his forehead, and gave him a roll with a seal upon it, which he told him to look at as he ran; and that he should turn it in at the celestial gate. So they went their way.

Then Christian gave three leaps for joy and went on, singing:

> Thus far did I come laden with my sin;
> Nor could aught ease the grief that I was in,
> Till I came hither: what a place is this!
> Must here be the beginning of my bliss?
> Must here the burden fall from off my back?
> Must here the strings that bound it to me crack?
> Blest cross! blest sepulchre! blest rather be
> The Man that was there put to shame for me!
>
> John Bunyan (1628–1688), *The Pilgrim's Progress*

4 *The music room*

The music of this Passion Chorale, enriched by the poignant harmonies of J. S. Bach, is a perfect interpretation of the words which take us into the heart of Christ's suffering.

> O sacred head, surrounded
>   By crown of piercing thorn!
> O bleeding head, so wounded,
>   So shamed and put to scorn!
> Death's pallid hue comes o'er thee,
>   The glow of life decays;
> Yet angel-hosts adore thee,
>   And tremble as they gaze.
>
> Thy comeliness and vigour
>   Is withered up and gone,
> And in thy wasted figure
>   I see death drawing on.
> O agony and dying!
>   O love to sinners free!

Jesu, all grace supplying,
  Turn thou thy face on me.

In this thy bitter Passion,
  Good Shepherd, think of me
With thy most sweet compassion,
  Unworthy though I be:
Beneath thy Cross abiding
  For ever would I rest,
In thy dear love confiding,
  And with thy presence blest.
            P. Gerhardt, based on *Salve caput cruentatum*,
                    translated by Sir H. W. Baker

5 *The quiet room*

Contemplate the cross, either in your imagination with
your eyes closed, or by fixing your gaze on a crucifix or the
cross made by the window lights or door or piece of
furniture. Look to the cross as the source of healing. Or you
may want to read an account of the crucifixion – Matthew
27: 32–56

* * * *

When I survey the wondrous Cross
  On which the Prince of Glory died,
My richest gain I count but loss,
  And pour contempt on all my pride.

Forbid it, Lord, that I should boast
  Save in the Cross of Christ my God;
All the vain things that charm me most,
  I sacrifice them to his Blood.

See from his head, his hands, his feet,
  Sorrow and love flow mingling down;
Did e'er such love and sorrow meet,
  Or thorns compose so rich a crown?

Were the whole realm of nature mine,
  That were an offering far too small;
Love so amazing, so divine,
  Demands my soul, my life, my all.
              Isaac Watts (1674–1748)

O Saviour of the world, who by thy Cross and
　　precious Blood hast redeemed us,
save us, and help us, we humbly beseech thee, O
　　Lord.

Visitation of the Sick, BCP

* 　* 　* 　*

God, the God I love and worship, reigns in sorrow
　　on the Tree,
Broken, bleeding, but unconquered; Very God of
　　God to me,
In a manger, in a cottage, in an honest workman's
　　shed,
In the homes of humble peasants and the simple
　　lives they lead;
In the life of One, an outcast and a vagabond on
　　earth,
In the common things He valued and proclaimed
　　of countless worth;
And above all, in the horror of the cruel death He
　　died,
Thou hast bid us seek Thy glory in the criminal
　　crucified;
And we find it – for Thy glory is the glory of love's
　　loss,
And Thou hast no other splendour than the
　　splendour of the Cross.

G. A. Studdert-Kennedy, (Quoted by Leslie
Weatherhead in A Private House of Prayer)

6 *The living room*

Prayer Beneath The Cross

My God, my Father, help me to pray
　　WITH JESUS ON THE CROSS.

By praying for any enemies
　　　who wish me hurt;
　　and more, for thine,
　　　who do injustice and cruelty on the earth.
Father, forgive them, for they know not what they do.

By praying for the guilty and condemned,
    WITH JESUS ON THE CROSS:
  for all facing trial or in prison,
    and all captives of sin:
bring them to look up to his holy Cross:
  and, hand in hand with him, go free.

By praying for the grace of love in human homes:
  for heavenly concord in thy household, the
    Church,
    born of Christ's blood:
praying with Jesus, with his Mother, with St
  John,
    for love, for holier love, on earth.

By holding fast to thee, my God, my God,
  who holdest fast to us,
in the black and desperate day
  and in the hour of death.

By praying, O Eternal Compassion,
  for all in pain of body or mind:
for souls that thirst for thee:
and souls that wander in dry places,
  seeking rest, but not seeking thee.

By praying for the present help of thine own Spirit,
  that all thou givest me to do
    may be fearlessly begun,
    and faithfully finished.

So help me God to pray WITH JESUS ON THE
  CROSS
and to commend my body, mind, and spirit,
O Father, into thy hands
  for life, for death, for time without
    end.   Amen.
    Eric Milner-White, *My God, My Glory* (56), SPCK 1954

7 *The door into the world*

We have eyes for looking, and our gaze needs to linger on
the face of Jesus on the cross.
        Brother Roger of Taizé, *The Way of the Cross*,
        p 52, Mowbray 1986

And now, O Father in heaven,
we entrust ourselves to you;
that living or dying,
joyful or suffering,
we may ever be with our Lord Jesus,
safe in your eternal care.   Amen.

Roger Pickering, CPP 121

Christ crucified draw us to himself, to find in him a sure ground for faith, a firm support for hope, and the assurance of sins forgiven, and may the blessing of God almighty, the Father, the Son, and the Holy Spirit, be among us, and remain with us always.   Amen.

Blessing for Passiontide, ASB

EASTER

1 *The entrance to the house of God's glory*

Praise be to the God and Father of our Lord Jesus Christ!
In his great mercy he has given us new birth into a living
hope through the resurrection of Jesus Christ from the
dead, and into an inheritance that can never perish, spoil
or fade – kept in heaven for you, who through faith are
shielded by God's power until the coming of the salvation that is ready to be revealed in the last time.

1 Peter 1: 3–5

> Christians to the Paschal Victim
> Offer your thankful praises!
> A Lamb the sheep redeemeth:
> Christ, who only is sinless,
> Reconcileth sinners to the Father.
> Death and life have contended
> In that combat stupendous:
> The Prince of Life, who died, reigns immortal . . .
> Christ indeed from death is risen,
> Our new life obtaining:
> Have mercy, Victor King, ever reigning!
> > Victimae Paschali, Eleventh-Century Sequence

God our Father, may the whole world join in a hymn
of thanksgiving for the great love you have shown us
in Jesus Christ our Lord, risen from the dead, and may
our hearts and lives echo your praise, now and always.
Amen.

A Christian's Prayer Book, CPP 126

2 *The therapy room*

And this is the testimony: God has given us eternal life, and this life is in his Son. He who has the Son has life; he who does not have the Son of God does not have life.

1 John 5: 11f

Lord of all life and power,
who through the mighty resurrection of your Son
overcame the old order of sin and death
to make all things new in him:
grant that we, being dead to sin
and alive to you in Jesus Christ,
may reign with him in glory;
to whom with you and the Holy Spirit
be praise and honour, glory and might,
now and in all eternity.

Collect for Easter Day, ASB

Heavenly Father,
by the power of your Holy Spirit
you give to your faithful people
new life in the water of baptism.
Guide and strengthen us by that same Spirit,
that we who are born again
may serve you in faith and love,
and grow into the full stature of your Son Jesus
    Christ,
who is alive and reigns with you and the Holy
    Spirit,
one God now and for ever.   Amen.

Collect for Confirmation, ASB

'In every age, the man who has seen the risen Christ is the man with a mission; his true home is a missionary community; and God wills that through him others may be drawn into the fellowship.'

3 *The library*

The Easter life becomes a free hymn of praise to the Father in the midst of the sighing of creation in bondage

(Romans 8). In the midst of creation groaning in travail
the children of God display an unsuspected freedom,
which makes them cry Abba! Father! in spite of everything. They really have no reason for this at all, except for
their fellowship with Christ. Yet in that fellowship 'the
power of the resurrection' is always bound up with the
'fellowship of Christ's sufferings', and conversely so.
Thus the earnest of the new creation in the spirit of our
freedom to believe leads us deeper than ever into solidarity with the sufferings of the world. So the 'power of
the resurrection', as Paul calls freedom, makes us followers of the crucified and leads us into fellowship with
the forsaken whose brother the crucified has become.
This may sound like a contradiction but is in fact an
inescapable correlation. Only those who are capable of
joy can feel pain at their own and other people's suffering. A man who can laugh can also weep. A man who has
hope is able to endure the world and to mourn . . .

Thus both the laughter of Easter and the sorrow of the
cross are alive in liberated men. They are not only
laughing with those who laugh and weeping with those
who weep, as Paul proposes in Romans 12: 15, but they
are also laughing with the weeping and weeping with the
laughing as the Beatitudes of Jesus recommended.

Jürgen Moltmann, *Theology and Joy*, p 52f, SCM Press 1973

4 *The music room*

JESUS lives! thy terrors now
  Can no more, O death appal us;
Jesus lives! by this we know
  Thou, O grave, canst not enthral us.
                              Alleluia!

Jesus lives! henceforth is death
  But the gate of life immortal:
This shall calm our trembling breath,
  When we pass its gloomy portal.
                              Alleluia!

Jesus lives! for us he died;
  Then, alone to Jesus living,

Pure in heart may we abide,
  Glory to our Saviour giving.
                    Alleluia!

Jesus lives! our hearts know well
  Naught from us his love shall sever;
Life nor death nor powers of hell
  Tear us from his keeping ever.
                    Alleluia!

Jesus lives! to him the throne
  Over all the world is given:
May we go where he is gone,
  Rest and reign with him in heaven.
                    Alleluia!
              C. F. Gellert, AMR 140

5 *The quiet room*

To-day the demand is (for a) spiritual resurrection: it is
under God – *the creating of life.* To confront a bewildered
and dishevelled age with the fact of Christ, to thrust upon
its confusion the creative word of the Cross and smite its
disenchantment with the glory of the Resurrection – this
is the urgent, overruling task. 'Son of man, can these
bones live?'

There is, therefore, no place to-day for a Church that is
not aflame with the Spirit who is the Lord and Giver of
life, nor any value in a theology which is not passionately
missionary. If there throbs through the Church the vitality of a living union with Christ – and apart from this the
Church has no claim to exist, no right to preach, it is
merely cumbering the ground – if the Church can indeed
say 'It is not I who live, it is Christ who lives in me,' then
the dark demonic forces of the age have met their match,
and the thrust of life is stronger than the drift of death. A
Church that knows its Lord and is possessed by its
Gospel cannot but propagate creatively the life that it has
found. A Christian who is taking his faith seriously
cannot but evangelize.

James S. Stewart, *A Faith to Proclaim*, Hodder 1953

*   *   *   *

When we received the new life of Christ at our baptism, we were 'partakers' in 'the creative word of the Cross' and in 'the glory of the Resurrection'. 'The vitality of a living union with Christ' throbbed through us.

Can we still say with St Paul 'It is not I who live, it is Christ who lives in me'?

If we can say this and know that His new life throbs in us, then we cannot help being a missionary and evangelist.

* * * *

Prayer: Risen Lord, send me someone today with whom I can share the new life you have given me in your Resurrection. Amen.

6 *The living room*

THOU ART RISEN, O LORD!
   Let the gospel trumpets speak,
and the news as of holy fire,
      burning and flaming and inextinguishable,
         run to the ends of the earth.

THOU ART RISEN, O LORD!
   Let all creation greet the good tidings
            with jubilant shout;
      for its redemption has come,
      the long night is past, the Saviour lives!
      and rides and reigns in triumph
            now and unto the age of ages.

THOU ART RISEN, O LORD!
   Let the quiet Altar dazzle with light;
      let us haste to thy Presence
      wondering, incredulous for joy;
            and partake of thy Risen Life.

THOU ART RISEN, MY LORD AND MY GOD!
   Rise up, my heart, give thanks, rejoice!
   And do thou, O Lord, deign to enter it
            despite the shut doors.
   Shew me thy hands and thy side,
            that it is thou thyself.
   Send me about thy business,

servant of the living King, the King of kings;
and hide my life in thine
    for ever and ever. Amen.
Eric Milner-White, *My God, My Glory*, SPCK 1954, 58

7 *The door into the world*

As they approached the village to which they were going,
Jesus acted as if he were going further. But they urged
him strongly, 'Stay with us, for it is nearly evening; the
day is almost over.' So he went in to stay with them.

When he was at the table with them, he took bread,
gave thanks, broke it and began to give it to them. Then
their eyes were opened and they recognised him, and he
disappeared from their sight. They asked each other,
'Were not our hearts burning within us while he talked
with us on the road and opened the Scriptures to us?'

They got up and returned at once to Jerusalem. There
they found the Eleven and those with them, assembled
together and saying, 'It is true! The Lord has risen and
has appeared to Simon.' Then the two told what had
happened on the way, and how Jesus was recognised by
them when he broke the bread.

Luke 24: 28–35

Risen Lord, who on the first Easter day drew near to your
two disciples on the Emmaus road, and at evening stayed
with them in their village home: be our unseen companion along the daily journey of our life, and at the
ending of the day come and abide with us in our
dwellings; for your love's sake. Amen.

Frank Colquhoun, CPP 137

*Note: the word 'companion' means someone with whom one shares
    bread.*

The God of peace, who brought again from the dead our
Lord Jesus, that great shepherd of the sheep, make *us*
perfect in every good work to do his will: and the blessing
of God almighty, the Father, the Son, and the Holy Spirit,
be among *us* and remain with *us* always. Amen.

Adapted from the Easter blessing, ASB *See* Hebrews 13: 20f

ASCENSION

1 *The entrance to the house of God's glory*

Lift up your heads, O you gates;
    lift them up, you ancient doors,
    that the King of glory may come in.
Who is he, this King of glory?
    The LORD Almighty –
    he is the King of glory.

Psalm 24: 9, 10

HAIL the day that sees him rise,
                Alleluia!
To his throne above the skies;
                Alleluia!
Christ, the Lamb for sinners given,
                Alleluia!
Enters now the highest heaven.
                Alleluia!

There for him high triumph waits;
                Alleluia!
Lift your heads, eternal gates!
                Alleluia!
He hath conquered death and sin;
                Alleluia!
Take the King of Glory in!
                Alleluia!

See! he lifts his hands above;
                Alleluia!
See! he shews the prints of love;
                Alleluia!
Hark! his gracious lips bestow,
                Alleluia!
Blessings on his Church below.
                Alleluia!

Still for us he intercedes,
                    Alleluia!
His prevailing Death he pleads;
                    Alleluia!
Near himself prepares our place,
                    Alleluia!
He the first-fruits of our race.
                    Alleluia!
                    AMR 147

Almighty God,
as we believe your only-begotten Son our Lord
    Jesus Christ
to have ascended into the heavens,
so may we also in heart and mind thither ascend
and with him continually dwell;
who is alive and reigns with you and the Holy
    Spirit,
one God, now and for ever.
                    Collect for Ascension Day, BCP and ASB

2 *The therapy room*

JESUS, our ascended and exalted Lord,
to whom has been given the name above all names:
    we worship and adore you.

Jesus, King of righteousness, King of peace,
enthroned at the right hand of the Majesty on high:
    we worship and adore you.

Jesus, our great High Priest, our Advocate with the
    Father,
who lives for ever to make intercession for us:
    we worship and adore you.

Jesus, the Pioneer of our salvation,
bringing many sons to glory through your passion:
    we worship and adore you.

'To him who sits on the throne and to the Lamb,
be praise and honour and glory and power,
    for ever and ever!'
                    Frank Colquhoun, NPP 134

JESUS, ascended Lord, focus our eyes on your
    glory.
Jesus, King of righteousness, heal all our
    relationships.
Jesus, our great High Priest, help us to rely more
            on your eternal and healing prayer for us.
Jesus, Pioneer of salvation, we thank you that you
            are ever bringing us your saving health.
Yours is the Kingdom, the power, and the glory,
            for ever and ever.   Amen.

3 The library

Today's readings are both taken from St Luke's writings:
the first from the close of his first volume; the second from
the opening of his second:

When he had led them out to the vicinity of Bethany,
he lifted up his hands and blessed them. While he was
blessing them, he left them and was taken up into
heaven. Then they worshipped him and returned to
Jerusalem with great joy. And they stayed continually at
the temple, praising God.

Luke 24: 50–53

*   *   *   *

In my former book, Theophilus, I wrote about all that
Jesus began to do and teach until the day he was taken up
to heaven, after giving instructions through the Holy
Spirit to the apostles he had chosen. After his suffering,
he showed himself to these men and gave many convinc-
ing proofs that he was alive. He appeared to them over a
period of forty days and spoke about the kingdom of
God. On one occasion, while he was eating with them, he
gave them this command: 'Do not leave Jerusalem, but
wait for the gift my Father promised, which you have
heard me speak about. For John baptised with water, but
in a few days you will be baptised with the Holy Spirit.'

So when they met together, they asked him, 'Lord, are you at this time going to restore the kingdom to Israel?'

He said to them: 'It is not for you to know the times or dates the Father has set by his own authority. But you will receive power when the Holy Spirit comes on you; and you will be my witnesses in Jerusalem, and in all Judea and Samaria, and to the ends of the earth.'

After he said this, he was taken up before their very eyes, and a cloud hid him from their sight.

They were looking intently up into the sky as he was going, when suddenly two men dressed in white stood beside them. 'Men of Galilee,' they said, 'why do you stand here looking into the sky? This same Jesus, who has been taken from you into heaven, will come back in the same way you have seen him go into heaven.'

Then they returned to Jerusalem from the hill called the Mount of Olives, a Sabbath day's walk from the city.

Acts 1: 1–12

*   *   *   *

Let us spend a few silent moments 'on the mount of the Ascension', before we return 'to the city' to await the Father's promised gift, the healing gift of the Holy Spirit.

*   *   *   *

4 *The music room*

SEE the Conqueror mounts in triumph,
    See the King in royal state
Riding on the clouds his chariot
    To his heavenly palace gate;
Hark! the choirs of angel voices
    Joyful Alleluias sing,
And the portals high are lifted
    To receive their heavenly King.

Who is this that comes in glory,
    With the trump of jubilee?
Lord of battles, God of armies,
    He has gained the victory;

He who on the Cross did suffer,
  He who from the grave arose,
He has vanquished sin and Satan,
  He by death has spoiled his foes.

He has raised our human nature
  On the clouds to God's right hand;
There we sit in heavenly places,
  There with him in glory stand:
Jesus reigns, adored by angels;
  Man with God is on the throne;
Mighty Lord, in thine Ascension
  We by faith behold our own.
    Christopher Wordsworth (1807–1885), AMR 148

5 *The quiet room*

As we recall the words we read in the library, let us use one
of Cardinal Newman's meditations on the Ascension:

My Lord, I follow Thee up to heaven; as Thou goest up,
my heart and mind go with Thee. Never was triumph like
this . . .

O memorable day! The Apostles feel it to be so, now
that it has come, though they felt so differently before it
came. When it was coming they dreaded it. They could
not think but it would be a great bereavement; but now,
as we read, they returned to Jerusalem 'with great joy'. O
what a time of triumph! They understood it now. They
understood how weak it had been in them to grudge their
Lord and Master, the glorious Captain of their salvation,
the Champion and First Fruits of the human family, this
crown of His great work. It was the triumph of redeemed
man. It is the completion of his redemption. It was the
last act, making the whole sure, for now man is actually
in heaven. He has entered into possession of his inheritance. The sinful race has now one of its own children
there, its own flesh and blood, in the person of the
Eternal Son. O what a wonderful marriage between
heaven and earth! It began in sorrow; but now the long
travail of that mysterious wedding day is over; the marriage feast is begun; marriage and birth have gone

together; man is new born when Emmanuel enters
heaven . . .

Be it so, my Lord Jesus, I give myself wholly to
Thee.   Amen.

J. H. Newman (1801–1890), *Meditations and Devotions*,
pp 69, 74, first published 1893, Burns & Oates 1964

Thou art the King of glory, O Christ; thou art the
    everlasting
Son of the Father.
When thou tookest upon thee to deliver man, thou
    didst not abhor the Virgin's womb.
When thou hadst overcome the sharpness of
    death, thou didst open the kingdom of heaven to
    all believers.
Thou sittest at the right hand of God, in the glory
    of the Father.

Te Deum, BCP

6 *The living room*

Ascended Lord, King of the Universe and nations, I lift
up my heart for all who, in our national affairs, are
bearing a load of responsibility. In my praying help me to
set aside their political views, that with dispassionate
sincerity I may pray for them as men and women. In all
their ways grant them sincerity and a desire to act in the
highest interests of our dear land. And when the burden
seems too heavy and weariness overtakes both body and
mind, comfort and sustain them and those dear to them,
and restore them to serve you in all they do, with clearer
vision and heightened ideals, that they may help to make
our country the instrument of your will. I ask it in your
holy name of Jesus, my risen, ascended and glorified
Lord.   Amen.

Adapted from a prayer by Leslie Weatherhead,
A Private House of Prayer

O God, the Lord of all kings and kingdoms, let your
healing hand control the nations and order their doings
to the fulfilment of your purposes on earth. Strengthen

those who strive after fellowship and brotherhood, who labour to establish righteousness and peace; guide the hearts and minds of rulers and statesmen, that they may seek first your kingdom of justice and freedom for all peoples, both great and small; for the sake of our ascended Lord Jesus Christ, who reigns eternally with you and the Holy Spirit, one God, world without end. Amen.

Adapted from a prayer by Hugh Johnston, *The Prayer Manual*,
Mowbray 1961

7 *The door into the world*

Then the eleven disciples went to Galilee, to the mountain where Jesus had told them to go. When they saw him, they worshipped him; but some doubted. Then Jesus came to them and said, 'All authority in heaven and on earth has been given to me. Therefore go and make disciples of all nations, baptising them in the name of the Father and of the Son and of the Holy Spirit, and teaching them to obey everything I have commanded you. And surely I will be with you always, to the very end of the age.'

Matthew 28: 16–20

Lord, you have charged your Church to preach the Gospel to the whole creation, and to make disciples of all nations: inspire us with your Spirit and empower us by your presence as you send us out to preach and teach and heal, that we may not fail you in the fulfilment of your purpose and that your kingdom may come on earth, as it is in heaven. We join our prayer with your eternal intercession. Amen.

Adapted from a prayer by Frederick B. MacNutt,
The Prayer Manual, Mowbray 1961

Christ our King make *us* faithful and strong to do his will, that *we* may reign with him in glory; and the blessing of God almighty, the Father, the Son, and the Holy Spirit, be among *us*, and remain with *us* always. Amen.

Blessing for Ascension, ASB

PENTECOST

1 *The entrance to the house of God's glory*

Jesus said, 'I am going to send you what my Father has promised; but stay in the city until you have been clothed with power from on high.'

Luke 24: 49

If Jesus had any one mission, it was to bring the power and healing of *God's creative, loving Spirit* to bear upon the moral, mental, and physical illnesses of the people around him. It was a matter of rescuing man from a situation in which he could not help himself. Jesus disclosed a new power, a ladder to bring him out of the pit of his brokenness and sin.

Morton T. Kelsey, *Healing and Christianity*, SCM Press 1973

Come, Holy Spirit, and fill the hearts of your faithful people, and kindle within them the fire of your love.
Send forth your Spirit and they shall be made.
And you will renew the face of the earth.
Lord, may the Comforter who proceeds from you illuminate our minds and lead us as your Son has promised into all truth; through the same Jesus Christ our Lord.   Amen.

Antiphon for Pentecost

2 *The therapy room*

Without the Holy Spirit God is far away,
Christ stays in the past,
The Gospel is simply an organisation,
authority a matter of propaganda,

the liturgy is no more than an evolution,
Christian loving a slave morality.

But in the Holy Spirit
the cosmos is resurrected and grows
with the birth pangs of the Kingdom,
the Risen Christ is there,
the Gospel is the power of life,
the Church shows forth the life of the Trinity,
authority is a liberating science,
mission is a Pentecost,
the liturgy is both renewal and anticipation,
human action is deified.

> Metropolitan Ignatius of Latakia
> at the Uppsala Assembly of the WCC 1968,
> (Quoted by Bishop Michael Ramsey in
> *Holy Spirit*, SPCK 1977)

O God, may the fire of your Holy Spirit
consume in us all that displeases you;
and kindle in our hearts a burning zeal
for the service of your kingdom;
through Jesus Christ our Lord.   Amen.

> Adapted from an ancient collect, NPP 144

3 The library

For Paul the congregation is the place where the Spirit
manifests itself (1 Cor. 14) in an overflowing wealth of
spiritual powers (charismata). According to Old Testament prophecy the Spirit counts as being the gift of the
last days (Isaiah 44: 3; 63: 14; Ezekiel 36: 27; Zechariah 4:
6). In the messianic era not only the chosen prophets and
kings but the whole people of God will be filled by the
living force and newly creating power of God. According
to Joel 2: 28f., this is the beginning of the outpouring of
the Spirit of God 'on all flesh'. That means the new
creation of all things for the eternal life of the kingdom,
and it means at the same time the glorifying of God; for
God himself is present in the Spirit. By virtue of the Spirit
God himself takes up his dwelling in his creation . . .

The promise of Joel is fulfilled in what happened at

Pentecost (Acts 2: 14–21). The Spirit of the last days and the eschatalogical community of the saved belong together. The new people of God see themselves in their existence and form as being 'the creation of the Spirit', and therefore as the initial fulfilment of the new creation of all things and the glorification of God. The Spirit calls them into life; the Spirit gives the community the authority for its mission; the Spirit makes its living powers and the ministries that spring from them effective; the Spirit unites, orders and preserves it. It therefore sees itself and its powers and tasks as deriving from and existing in the eschatalogical history of the Spirit. In this it experiences not only what it itself is, but also where it belongs. It discovers the redeeming future of the world in the overriding span of the Spirit's history . . .

Paul talks about *charismata*, meaning the *energies* of the new life (1 Corinthians 12: 6, 11), which is to say the powers of the Spirit. These are designations of what is, not of what ought to be. They are the gifts of grace springing from the creative grace of God . . . Creative grace leads to new obedience; and the gifts of grace and the energies of the Spirit lead to ready, courteous service . . .

The charismata can be understood as the crystallization and individuation of the one charis given in Christ. Through the powers of the Spirit, the one Spirit gives every individual his specific share and calling, which is exactly cut out for him, in the process of the new creation. Because the word 'spirit' is exposed to traditional misunderstandings, we must remember that for Paul the Spirit is 'the power of the resurrection' and thus the divine power of creation and new creation (Romans 8: 11; Romans 4: 17). The Spirit is not an ideal, over against what is physical and mortal, but is God himself, who calls into being the thing that is not, makes the godless righteous, and raises the dead. He is the 'life-giving' Spirit, giving life to everything that is mortal (1 Corinthians 15: 45). The community's spiritual powers must be correspondingly understood as creative powers endowed with life. As the power of resurrection, the Spirit is the reviving presence of the future of eternal life in the midst of the history of death; he is the presence of the future of the new creation in the midst of the dying life of this world and its evil state. In the Spirit and through the Spirit's powers the eschatalogical new thing – 'Behold I make all things new' – becomes the new thing in history, reaching, at least in tendency, over the whole breadth of creation in its present wretchedness.

Jürgen Moltmann, *The Church in the Power of the Spirit*,
SCM Press 1975

4 *The music room*

Veni, Creator Spiritus

Come, Holy Ghost, our souls inspire,
And lighten with celestial fire.
Thou the anointing Spirit art,
Who dost thy seven-fold gifts impart.

Thy blessed Unction from above,
Is comfort, life, and fire of love.
Enable with perpetual light
The dullness of our blinded sight.

Anoint and cheer our soiled face
With the abundance of thy grace.
Keep far our foes, give peace at home;
Where thou art guide, no ill can come.

Teach us to know the Father, Son,
And thee, of both, to be but One.
That, through the ages all along,
This may be our endless song:

Praise to thy eternal merit,
Father, Son, and Holy Spirit.   Amen.

Before the 10th century; translation by
Bishop Cosin (1594–1672)

The music for this ancient hymn is one of the best known of all plainsong melodies. The setting by Thomas Attwood is also particularly fine.

5 *The quiet room*

> When the day of Pentecost came, they were all together
> in one place. Suddenly a sound like the blowing of a
> violent wind came from heaven and filled the whole
> house where they were sitting. They saw what seemed to
> be tongues of fire that separated and came to rest on each
> of them. All of them were filled with the Holy Spirit . . .
>
> Acts 2: 1–4

Let us keep this picture in our minds and ponder the
implications of 'a return to the New Testament concept
of the Spirit-filled and Spirit-led group living in the
continual forgiveness of God the life of the new mankind,
and offering a body in which Christ can be incarnate still, to
heal and reconcile and liberate.'

* * * *

This was how Bishop John V. Taylor saw, and at times
witnessed, the rediscovery of healing today, as he wrote in
The Go-Between God, SCM Press 1972. He went on to quote a
doctor who looked to the Church to find a loving and
accepting community such as he had experienced in a
mental hospital.

'Should not the Church fellowship be a therapeutic community based upon the free flow of Christian love? Should
it not be providing the kind of atmosphere in which people
are free to be themselves and to find healing in the redemptive nature of an accepting sacrificial love, the love of God,
mediated by the members of the Church? Dare we share the
life of Jesus together like this in our Church fellowships and
let this love expose our badness to the full, knowing that he
loves us just the same, or must we fall back on the more
comfortable path of good works and respectable Christian
behaviour?'

* * * *

May our church, our community, our home, be a
fellowship of the Holy Spirit.　Amen.

6 The living room

Prayer to the Holy Ghost

O Holy Ghost, Paraclete, perfect in us the work begun by Jesus: enable us to continue to pray fervently in the name of the whole world: hasten in every one of us the growth of a profound interior life; give vigour to our apostolate so that it may reach all men and all peoples, all redeemed by the Blood of Christ and all belonging to him. Mortify in us our natural pride, and raise us to the realms of holy humility, of the real fear of God, of generous courage. Let no earthly bond prevent us from honouring our vocation, no cowardly consideration disturb the claims of justice, no meanness confine the immensity of charity within the narrow bounds of petty selfishness. Let everything in us be on a grand scale: the search for truth and the devotion to it, and readiness for self-sacrifice, even to the cross and death; and may everything finally be according to the last prayer of the Son to his heavenly Father, and according to your Spirit, O Holy Spirit of love, which the Father and the Son desired to be poured out over the Church and its institutions, over the souls of men and over nations. Amen. Amen. Alleluia, Alleluia!

Pope John XXIII from his homily for Pentecost, Sunday June 10th, 1962, *Journey of a Soul*, Geoffrey Chapman 1964

O God, empty us of self
    and fill us with your Holy Spirit,
that we may bring forth abundantly
    the fruit of love, joy and peace,
and glorify you day by day
    in lives renewed in the beauty of holiness;
through Jesus Christ our Lord.   Amen.

Frank Colquhoun, CPP 167

7 The door into the world

'You will receive power when the Holy Spirit comes on you; and you will be my witnesses in Jerusalem, and in all Judea and Samaria, and to the ends of the earth.'

Acts 1: 8

Almighty God,
who on the day of Pentecost
sent your Holy Spirit to the disciples
with the wind from heaven and in tongues of
    flame,
filling them with joy and boldness to preach the
    Gospel:
send us out in the power of the same Spirit
to witness to your truth
and to draw all men to the fire of your love;
through Jesus Christ our Lord.   Amen.

Second collect for Pentecost, ASB

The grace of our Lord Jesus Christ, and the love of God, and the fellowship of the Holy Spirit, be with us all evermore.   Amen.

2 Corinthians 13: 14

ST LUKE AND ALL SAINTS

1 *The entrance to the house of God's glory*

We praise thee, O God: we acknowledge thee to be
the Lord.
All the earth doth worship thee: the Father
everlasting.
To thee all Angels cry aloud: the Heavens, and all
the Powers therein.
To thee, Cherubin, and Seraphin: continually do
cry,
Holy, Holy, Holy: Lord God of Sabaoth;
Heaven and earth are full of the Majesty: of thy
Glory.
The glorious company of the Apostles: praise thee.
The goodly fellowship of the Prophets: praise thee.
The noble army of Martyrs: praise thee.
The holy Church throughout all the world: doth
acknowledge thee:
The Father: of an infinite Majesty;
Thine honourable, true: and only Son;
Also the Holy Ghost: the Comforter.
Thou art the King of Glory: O Christ.
Thou art the everlasting Son: of the Father.
When thou tookest upon thee to deliver man: thou
didst not abhor the Virgin's womb.
When thou hadst overcome the sharpness of
death: thou didst open the Kingdom of Heaven
to all believers.
Thou sittest at the right hand of God; in the Glory
of the Father.
We believe that thou shalt come: to be our Judge.
We therefore pray thee, help thy servants: whom
thou hast redeemed with thy precious blood.

Make them to be numbered with thy Saints: in
    glory everlasting.

Te Deum, BCP

Almighty God,
who inspired Luke the physician
to proclaim the love and healing power of your
    Son:
give your Church, by the grace of the Spirit
    and through the medicine of the gospel,
the same love and power to heal;
through Jesus Christ our Lord.

Collect for St Luke, ASB

2 *The therapy room*

Great friends, great fellowship of God,
        praise God on my behalf,
    so low, so little is my own power of praise.
You who were penitent and watched in prayer,
    laboured, held fast, and overcame,
        lend to my would-be praises the voice of yours!
You, whose days were humbly hid in Jesus,
    who kept his words and works unto the end,
        you who were faithful unto death;
You, clothed now in white raiment
    and crowned with life;
You, going forth conquering and to conquer
        after the King of kings –
cry out for all the heavens, for all Holy Church,
        and for me, a sinner,
            Alleluia, Alleluia.
            Eric Milner-White, *My God, My Glory*, p 66

3 *The library*

Jesus, seeing the multitudes, went up into a mountain;
and when he was set, his disciples came unto him. And
he opened his mouth, and taught them, saying,

Blessed are the poor in spirit: for theirs is the
kingdom of heaven.
Blessed are they that mourn: for they shall be
comforted.
Blessed are the meek: for they shall inherit the
earth.
Blessed are they which do hunger and thirst after
righteousness: for they shall be filled.
Blessed are the merciful: for they shall obtain
mercy.
Blessed are the pure in heart: for they shall see
God.
Blessed are the peace-makers: for they shall be
called the children of God.
Blessed are they which are persecuted for
righteousness' sake: for theirs is the kingdom of
heaven.
Blessed are ye, when men shall revile you, and
persecute you, and shall say all manner of evil
against you falsely for my sake.
Rejoice, and be exceeding glad; for great is your
reward in heaven: for so persecuted they the
prophets which were before you.
The Gospel for All Saints Day, Book of Common Prayer,
Matthew 5: 1–12

* * * *

Blessed are the eyes that see
The things that you have seen,
Blessed are the feet that walk
The ways where you have been.

Blessed are the eyes that see
The Agony of God,
Blessed are the feet that tread
The paths his feet have trod.

Blessed are the souls that solve
The paradox of Pain,
And find the path that, piercing it,
Leads through to Peace again.
G. A. Studdert Kennedy (1883–1929)

4 *The music room*

For all the Saints who from their labours rest,
Who thee by faith before the world confest,
Thy name, O Jesu, be for ever blest.
Alleluya!

Thou wast their Rock, their Fortress, and their
  Might;
Thou, Lord, their Captain in the well-fought fight;
Thou in the darkness drear their one true Light.
Alleluya!

O may thy soldiers, faithful, true, and bold,
Fight as the Saints who nobly fought of old,
And win, with them, the victor's crown of gold.
Alleluya!

O blest communion! fellowship divine!
We feebly struggle, they in glory shine;
Yet all are one in thee, for all are thine.
Alleluya!

And when the strife is fierce, the warfare long,
Steals on the ear the distant triumph-song,
And hearts are brave again, and arms are strong.
Alleluya!

The golden evening brightens in the west;
Soon, soon to faithful warriors cometh rest:
Sweet is the calm of Paradise the blest.
Alleluya!

But lo! there breaks a yet more glorious day;
The Saints triumphant rise in bright array:
The King of glory passes on his way.
Alleluya!

From earth's wide bounds, from ocean's farthest
  coast,
Through gates of pearl streams in the countless
  host,
Singing to Father, Son, and Holy Ghost.
Alleluya!
Bishop W. W. How (1823–97), EH 641

It is fitting that one of our country's greatest composers, Ralph Vaughan Williams, has written the tune indelibly associated with this hymn, 'Sine Nomine'. Bishop Walsham How was the first bishop of Wakefield.

5 *The quiet room*

In his gospel, Luke is quite certain of the way in which Jesus commissioned his disciples. He gave them specific orders. Luke is equally certain that these orders were carried out:

> When Jesus had called the Twelve together, he gave them power and authority to drive out all demons and to cure diseases, and he sent them out to preach the kingdom of God and to heal the sick . . .
> So they set out and went from village to village, preaching the gospel and healing people everywhere.
> Luke 9: 1, 2, 6

How obedient have we been to this commission?
Is my church fulfilling this commission today?

* * * *

In his second volume, the Acts of the Apostles, Luke again assures us that the Apostles kept on being faithful to this commission. Chapters 3 and 4 are given over to proving this and he has more to say in the next chapter:

> The apostles performed many miraculous signs and wonders among the people. And all the believers used to meet together in Solomon's Colonnade. No-one else dared join them, even though they were highly regarded by the people. Nevertheless, more and more men and women believed in the Lord and were added to their number. As a result, people brought the sick into the streets and laid them on beds and mats so that at least Peter's shadow might fall on some of them as he passed by. Crowds gathered also from the towns around Jerusalem bringing their sick and those tormented by evil spirits, and all of them were healed.
> Acts 5: 12–16

Two thousand years later, the methods may be different, but the power and authority are still the same. Signs and wonders do happen among our sick folk in answer to prayer and ministry.

* * * *

Lord, look upon this work, and enable your sevants to speak your word with great boldness. Stretch out your hand to heal and perform miraculous signs and wonders through the name of your holy servant Jesus.   Amen.

Acts 4: 29, 30

6 *The living room*

A Doctor's Prayer

O Lord Jesus Christ,
anoint me this day, with Your Heavenly grace,
for all my dealings with Your people:
Anoint me with Your Heavenly wisdom;
Your true love, and Your enduring patience.
In abandonment may I be stripped of all
    non-essentials,
to learn Your true priorities for others;
In agonising may I let go,
and learn a new experience of You in others;
In awaiting may I hunger and thirst after You,
and be Yourself with others;
In adoring may I be captivated by Your love,
the God who IS, through others.
O Lord Jesus Christ,
in Whose presence is stillness and true healing,
may I in all these ways be Your wounded healer,
and live to-day for all those in my care.
For the glory of Your Name, and the furtherance of
    Your Kingdom.   Amen.

Maro Laxton

7 The door into the world

Therefore, since we are surrounded by such a great cloud of witnesses, let us throw off everything that hinders and the sin that so easily entangles, and let us run with perseverance the race marked out for us. Let us fix our eyes on Jesus, the author and perfecter of our faith, who for the joy set before him endured the cross, scorning its shame, and sat down at the right hand of the throne of God.

Hebrews 12: 1, 2

Almighty God, you have surrounded us with a great cloud of witnesses: Grant that we, encouraged by the good example of your servant Luke, the beloved physician, and all the Saints, may persevere in running the race that is set before us, until at last we may with them attain to your eternal joy; through Jesus Christ, the pioneer and perfecter of our faith, who lives and reigns with you and the Holy Spirit, one God, for ever and ever. Amen.

The Prayer Book of the American Episcopal Church, Church Hymnal Corporation and Seabury Press 1977

May God give us grace to follow St Luke and all his saints in faith and hope and love, and may the blessing of God Almighty, the Father, the Son, and the Holy Spirit, be upon us this day and all our days. Amen.

Adapted from the blessing for Saints' Days, ASB

SPARE
ROOMS

SPARE ROOMS

Litany of Healing

Let us name before God those for whom we offer our prayers . . .

God the Father, your will for all people is health
and salvation;
We praise you and thank you, O Lord.

God the Son, you came that we might have life,
and might have it more abundantly;
We praise you and thank you, O Lord.

God the Holy Spirit, you make our bodies the
temple of your presence;
We praise you and thank you, O Lord.

Holy Trinity, one God, in you we live and move
and have our being;
We praise you and thank you, O Lord.

Lord, grant your healing grace to all who are sick,
injured, or disabled, that they may be made
whole;
Hear us, O Lord of life.

Grant to all who seek your guidance, and to all
who are lonely, anxious, or despondent, a
knowledge of your will and an awareness of
your presence;
Hear us, O Lord of life.

Mend broken relationships, and restore those in
emotional distress to soundness of mind and
serenity of spirit;
Hear us, O Lord of life.

Bless physicians, nurses, and all others who
   minister to the suffering, granting them wisdom
   and skill, sympathy and patience;
Hear us, O Lord of life.

Grant to the dying peace and a holy death, and
   uphold by the grace and consolation of your
   Holy Spirit those who are bereaved;
Hear us, O Lord of life.

Restore to wholeness whatever is broken by
   human sin, in our lives, in our nation, and in the
   world;
Hear us, O Lord of life.

You are the Lord who does wonders:
You have declared your power among the peoples.

With you, O Lord, is the well of life:
And in your light we see light.

Hear us, O Lord of life:
Heal us, and make us whole.

Let us pray.
A period of silence may follow here.

Concluding Prayers
Almighty God, giver of life and health: Send your blessing on all who are sick, and upon those who minister to
them, that all weakness may be vanquished by the
triumph of the risen Christ; who lives and reigns for ever
and ever.   Amen.

Heavenly Father, you have promised to hear what we ask
in the Name of your son: Accept and fulfil our petitions,
we pray, not as we ask in our ignorance, nor as we
deserve in our sinfulness, but as you know and love us in
your Son Jesus Christ our Lord.   Amen.

O Lord our God, accept the fervent prayers of your
people; in the multitude of your mercies look with compassion upon us and all who turn to you for help, for you
are gracious, O lover of souls, and to you we give glory,
Father, Son, and Holy Spirit, now and for ever.   Amen.

The Grace

The Book of Occasional Services, Church Hymnal Corporation,
            New York (Copyright Church Pension Fund, 1979)

A Doctor's Prayer Poem

Our dear Lord sent out His disciples
To anoint with Oil in His Name,
To preach the Good News of His Kingdom,
The power of Love to proclaim!

They gladly went forth to obey Him
For such was their trust in His Love;
Their faith was then quickly rewarded,
As so many events were to prove.

They returned in such joy to the Master
With stories and tales to relate
Of healings and blessings abundant –
Wide open had been Heaven's Gate!

Today, as you kneel in the chapel
That same Sacrament to receive,
Borne by the prayers of believers,
Look up in His Face – and believe!

The Oil, in the outward Anointing,
Brings Christ's Spirit right into your heart,
And He, who created and loves you,
Knows how to repair each hurt part.

Over chaos the Spirit once hovered,
Out of chaos such beauty was brought;
How much more will He now re-create you
In Christ's likeness – so perfectly wrought.

Then having received such great blessing
At the Hands of God's chosen Priest,
Go out to the world in His Power,
For *you* – are the Body of Christ!

Elizabeth Davies, written for a fellow retreatant
who was to be anointed

'The Afterglow'

Blessed are you now,
Who receive His gift
From His own anointed hands;

Outpoured in the Trinity's immeasurable, precious
   gift
To His faithful servants:
Fulfilment in the inmost souls, perfect Love,
Sufficient Sacrifice; His Kingdom within us.

His Kingdom within us by His design –
Home wholly of prayer and peace
Spreading its vision to all around –
Until all mankind is reborn
Into His wholesome Love. Alleluia!   Amen.

Hedi Limebury

A Prayer for Healing After a Broken Relationship

'O my Lord – Wash me,
        Wash me of this relationship;
    Wash me of the pain of it,
    Wash me of the hurt of it,
    Wash me of the disappointment of it,
    Wash me of the resentment of it,
    Wash me of the attachment to it,
    Wash me of the hurtful memories of it
    That come back in quietness, and in prayer time,
    That come back in the silent night hours
    And rend my body and very heart
    With an agony of writhing tears.

    I give myself into Your hands, Lord,
    O Wash me, as I lie still before You.
    Do for me what I cannot do for myself.
        Heal me, Lord . . .
    Under Your healing touch
    Hour by hour, and day by day
    I shall be set free, until
    the intention of my heart is pure love,
    And until all my actions give Your lovely Name
    the glory that can flow from a pure
        heart.'   Amen.

Anonymous

The World's Pain

> O Lord,
>   so many sick
>   so many starving
>   so many deprived
>   so many sad
>   so many bitter
>   so many fearful.
> When I look at them
>   my heart fails,
> When I look at You
>   I hope again.
> Help me to help You
>   to reduce the world's pain.
> O God of infinite Compassion
> O ceaseless Energy of love.   Amen.
>
> George Appleton

The Prayer and Ministry of a Hospital Chaplain

In God's holy name, Father, Son and Holy Spirit.   Amen.

> O Lord, our heavenly Father,
> behold, visit, and relieve this your son/daughter.
> Look upon *him* with your eyes of mercy,
> give *him* comfort and sure confidence in you,
> defend *him* from all illness,
> and keep *him* in your peace, care,
> love and safety. This we pray in the
> power of the Holy Spirit and Jesus
> Christ our Lord.   Amen.
>
> Adapted from BCP

Following the rubric in the ASB *Ministry to the Sick* I then lay on hands using these words:

> In the name of our Lord Jesus Christ who laid his hands on the sick that they might be healed, *I* lay *my* hands upon you, *N.* May almighty God, Father, Son and Holy

Spirit, make you whole in body, mind, and spirit, give you light and peace, and keep you in life eternal. Amen.

If anointing is to follow I lay on hands in silence then follow the Roman Ritual for anointing with the following introduction:

My brothers and sisters: Our Lord Jesus Christ has told us through his apostle James: 'Is there anyone sick among you? Let him call for the elders of the Church, and let them pray over him and anoint him in the name of the Lord. This prayer, made in faith, will save the sick man. The Lord will restore his health, and if he has committed any sins, they will be forgiven.

Let us entrust our sick brother/sister
to the power and strength of Jesus Christ, that
Christ may ease his/her sufferings and grant
him/her health and salvation.

The Anointing
On the forehead 'Through this holy anointing may the Lord
in his love and mercy help you with the grace of the
Holy Spirit.'
Then on the hands 'May the Lord who frees you from sin
save you and raise you up.'
Then the prayer 'Lord Jesus Christ, you took our weakness
on yourself and bore our sufferings in your passion
and death.
Hear this prayer for our brother/sister N. You are
his/her Redeemer: strengthen his/her hope for salvation and in your kindness sustain him/her in body and
soul. You live and reign for ever and ever.   Amen.'
The Lord's Prayer
The Grace

Eucharistic Prayers

The Eucharist is the journey of the Church into the dimension of the Kingdom . . . the holding of the past and future in the now of faith.

Alexander Schmemann

The power of the Eucharist gives life to the body as well as the soul.

St Irenaeus (late 2nd century)

Christ is present in his timeless potency.

Michael Ramsey

Before receiving:
  Lord Jesus Christ, let not the partaking of your Body which I, though unworthy, do presume to receive, turn to my judgement and condemnation: but according to your loving-kindness, let it be profitable to me for the receiving of protection and healing both of body and soul: who with God the Father, in the unity of the Holy Spirit, lives and reigns, God, world without end. Amen.
After receiving:
  Grant, O Lord, that what we have taken with our lips we may receive with a pure heart: and may this temporal gift be to us an eternal healing.   Amen.

Prayers from the priest's private devotions

Almighty God,
we thank you for feeding us
with the body and blood of your Son Jesus Christ.
Through him we offer you our souls and bodies
to be a living sacrifice.
Send us out
in the power of your Spirit
to live and work
to your praise and glory. Amen.

The Order for Holy Communion Rite A, ASB

A Prayer for the Day

Lord, we offer to you ourselves this day,
      for the work you want accomplished,
      for the people you want us to meet,
      for the words you want to be uttered,
      for the silences you want to be kept,
      for the places you want us to enter,

for the new ways you want pioneered.
Go with us along the way, Lord,
and enable us to realise your presence,
at all times
and in all places
our living Lord Jesus Christ.   Amen.

M.M.

An Evening Hymn

AT even, ere the sun was set,
The sick, O Lord, around thee lay;
O in what divers pains they met!
O with what joy they went away!

Once more 'tis eventide, and we
Oppressed with various ills draw near;
What if thy form we cannot see?
We know and feel that thou art here.

O Saviour Christ, our woes dispel;
For some are sick, and some are sad,
And some have never loved thee well,
And some have lost the love they had;

And some have found the world is vain,
Yet from the world they break not free;
And some have friends who give them pain,
Yet have not sought a friend in thee;

And none, O Lord, have perfect rest,
For none are wholly free from sin;
And they who fain would serve thee best
Are conscious most of wrong within.

O Saviour Christ, thou too art Man;
Thou hast been troubled, tempted, tried;
Thy kind but searching glance can scan
The very wounds that shame would hide;

Thy touch has still its ancient power;
No word from thee can fruitless fall:
Hear, in this solemn evening hour,
And in thy mercy heal us all.

H. Twells, AMR 20

Healing and Peace at Bedtime

Jesus, through the power of the Holy Spirit,
  go back into my memory as I sleep.
Every hurt that has ever been done to me – heal
  that hurt.
Every hurt that I have ever caused to another
  person – heal that hurt.
All the relationships that have been damaged in
  my whole life of which I am unaware – heal
  those relationships.

But, Lord, if there is anything that I need to do – if I
  still need to go to a person because they are
  suffering from my hand, bring that person to my
  awareness.

I choose to forgive, and I ask to be forgiven,
Remove whatever bitterness may be in my heart,
  Lord, and fill the empty spaces with your love.

Thank you, Jesus.   Amen.
                                    Paddy and Betty Mitchell

Give me this night, O Father, the peace of mind
                which is truly rest.
Take from me
        All envy of anyone else
        All resentment for anything which has been
          withheld from me
        All bitterness against anyone who has hurt
          or wronged me
        All anger against the apparent injustices of
          life
        All foolish worry about the future and all
          futile regret about the past.
Help me to be
        At peace with myself
        At peace with my fellow human beings
        At peace with YOU
So indeed may I lay myself down to rest in peace,
        through Jesus Christ my Lord.   Amen.
                                    Roy Lawrence

Deep peace of the running wave to you,
Deep peace of the flowing air to you,
Deep peace of the quiet earth to you,
Deep peace of the shining stars to you,
Deep peace of the Son of Peace to you.
         A Celtic Christian Benediction

Copyrights

The author and publisher have endeavoured to trace all copyright holders for the material in this anthology but apologise for any inadvertent omissions which will be rectified in any reprint.

For permission to use copyright material they are grateful to the following sources:

The Alternative Service Book: Extracts from *The Alternative Service Book* 1980 and *Ministry to the Sick*, which are copyright © The Central Board of Finance of the Church of England, are reproduced with permission.

George Appleton, extracts from *Journey for a Soul*, Collins/Fontana; extracts from *One Man's Prayers*, the author and SPCK; extract taken from *Prayers from a Troubled Heart* by George Appleton published and copyright 1983 by Darton, Longman & Todd, London and is used by the permission of the publishers; extract from *The Quiet Heart*, William Collins Ltd.

Dr Marion Ashton, extract from *Growing into Wholeness*, Kingsway Publications 1985.

William Barclay, extracts from *Prayers for the Christian Year*, SCM Press Ltd.

Elizabeth Basset, extracts taken from *Love is My Meaning* edited by Elizabeth Basset published and copyright 1973 by Darton, Longman & Todd, London and are used by permission of the publishers.

Book of Common Prayer: extracts from the *Book of Common Prayer* 1662, which is Crown Copyright in the United Kingdom are reproduced by permission of Eyre & Spottiswoode (Publishers) Ltd, Her Majesty's Printers London.

C. H. Boutflower, 'O God in this thine hour of grace,' Hymn 460 from *Hymns Ancient and Modern Revised*, SPCK.

Christopher Bryant, extract taken from *Jung and the Christian Way* by Christopher Bryant published and copyright 1983 by Darton, Longman & Todd, London, is used by the permission of the publishers.

A. E. Campion, extracts from *Prayers for Christian Healing*, A. R. Mowbray & Co. Ltd.

Tony Castle, eleven prayers from *Hodder Book of Christian Prayers*, copyright © 1986 by Tony Castle, and three quotations from *Hodder Book of Christian Quotations*, copyright © 1982 by Tony Castle, reprinted by permission of Hodder and Stoughton Ltd.

Jean-Pierre de Caussade, extracts from *The Sacrament of the Present Moment*, translated by Kitty Muggeridge, Fount paperbacks, William Collins Ltd.

Index

JESUS – MAN OF PRAYER

Sister Margaret Magdalen

The primary purpose of Christ's prayer life was to glorify God. In this devotional reflection upon those passages in the Bible that reveal how Jesus prayed, Sister Margaret Magdalen analyses the Kingdom prayer Christ bequeathed to his disciples of all generations; his redemptive prayer in suffering, and the darkness and desolation he experienced prior to his death which is seen in conjunction with the prayer of commitment which completed his self-offering.

The place of contemplative wonder, solitude and silence in Christ's prayer life is examined, as is the importance he attached to the traditional liturgical prayers of the Jewish people and meditation on the Scripture.

Encouraging her readers to enter imaginatively into what prayer must have meant to Jesus, Sister Margaret Magdalen links Christ's actions and teachings on prayer with the experience and practice of spiritual writers through the ages. She examines the richness Christ's prayers have in Christian traditions including those of Evangelical, Catholic, Puritan, Protestant, Orthodox and Charismatic writers.

No reader will be able to remain unchallenged and unrenewed in his or her own prayer life.

Sister Margaret Magdalen is an Anglican nun, now living and working in Botswana.

THE HEALINGS OF JESUS

Michael Harper

Healing is a subject of increasing interest and endeavour in the Church today. Where better to place the current debate but firmly in the context of Jesus' healings as we read of them in the four Gospels?

In this comprehensive study, Michael Harper examines the historicity and meaning of miracles, looking at the place of healing in the Old Testament before examining its centrality in the Gospel of the Kingdom. The ministry of Jesus was a liberating one, opening the way to healing and wholeness in all aspects of life. Tackling such issues as that of deliverance — from Satan, sin and death — Michael Harper discerns the principles behind Jesus' healings and shows how they still apply today.

MICHAEL HARPER was the editor of *Renewal* magazine and is the author of *That We May Be One*, *Let my People Grow*, and *The Love Affair*.